HIGH PRAISE FOR
G. J. MEYER AND
EXECUTIVE BLUES

"AN ASTONISHING WORK. . . . The haunting, bitter sound of the jobless blues, sung by an ex-corporate executive. The disdain of the big boys for their own, suddenly redundant, is as corrosive as their contempt for Joe Six-Pack."—Studs Terkel

"A moral for employers: think again about firing an employee who has the talent to write about it and a penchant for sharp character sketches. Here's a funny, frank, and underlying it all, melancholy journal of a painful journey."—*Kirkus Reviews*

"A story which brings to life the dry news reports of corporate downsizing and restructuring—compelling in its honesty and detail, frightening as a reminder of the vulnerability of all employees in today's economy."—Charles Heckscher, author of *White Collar Blues*

"A book that will enlighten and amuse many, and shame those who ignored and humiliated him."—*Fortune*

Please turn the page for more extraordinary acclaim. . . .

EXECUTIVE BLUES

Down and Out in Corporate America

G.J. Meyer

A Dell Trade Paperback

A DELL TRADE PAPERBACK

Published by
Dell Publishing
a division of
Bantam Doubleday Dell Publishing Group, Inc.
1540 Broadway
New York, New York 10036

ISBN: 0-440-50765-0

Reprinted by arrangement with Franklin Square Press

Printed in the United States of America

Published simultaneously in Canada

October 1996

10   9   8   7   6   5   4   3   2   1

BVG

ACKNOWLEDGMENTS

This book would not exist without the encouragement, support, and counsel of Denise Shannon, Marguerite Biddle, and Regina Engelken. They are, however, responsible for none of its faults.

CONTENTS

PART I

Autumn 1991

The Best Thing That Ever Happened to Me

I'M NOT GETTING any interviews.

I call and call and call, looking for leads. But when I turn one up and send in my résumé, nothing comes back. When I follow the résumés with phone calls, secretaries get rid of me so smoothly that before I know what's happened I'm talking into a dead line.

This has been going on for weeks, and it's starting to scare me.

Then one afternoon the phone rings and it's a man I've been trying to reach, a headhunter named Roger Bullard in the Atlanta office of Russell Reynolds. He's looking for a p.r. vice president for Holiday Inns, Inc., he's seen my résumé, and he has nice things to say about it.

Would I rather meet him in New York or Atlanta? He has offices in both places.

"Your choice," I say. "I'd vote for New York." Offered a free trip, I'll take New York over Atlanta any day.

I wait while Bullard checks his calendar. "Monday in New York, then. Nine o'clock. Go ahead and make your reservations, and tomorrow call my secretary to confirm."

My wife, Pam, and our daughter, Sarah, have been standing behind me, listening to my half of the conversation. When I hang up they're all smiles. "Holiday Inns!" I say. "Monday in New York!" High fives all around.

First thing the next morning I talk with Bullard's secretary. I give her my flight number, tell her I'll be arriving at the Shelburne Murray Hill Hotel on Sunday evening. She gives me the Russell Reynolds address: Park Avenue. She reminds me to be there at nine.

The offices, when I arrive, are like something out of the London home of a maharaja. All the walls are paneled the expensive way, Sheraton furniture, thick rugs, gleaming parquet floors. I'm gleaming, too: shoes, collar, cuffs. The crease in my trousers could draw blood, and I'm feeling good about the fact that despite my nervousness I managed seven good hours of sleep and an early jog in Central Park.

A mirror near the elevator indicates that I don't look like what I am: out of work, a guy who has been thrown out of two corporations in the past three years, a little bitter, more than a little overeager.

I tell the receptionist that I'm there for an appointment with Mr. Bullard. With a slightly quizzical look she answers that he's not in yet, and I say I know I'm early. Moving delicately, not wanting to wrinkle the suit I've carried so carefully a thousand miles, I lower myself onto a leather sofa. Gingerly, keeping my fingertips clear of the ink, I open *The Wall Street Journal* on the coffee table in front of me and settle in to wait.

At nine the receptionist looks over at me, dials her phone, has a brief conversation I can't hear. She hangs up and looks at me again.

"You did say you have an appointment with Mr. Bullard?"

"Yes, I did. Nine o'clock."

"I'm sorry . . . but Mr. Bullard isn't scheduled to be in New York today."

When I call Atlanta, Bullard's secretary sounds almost as shocked as I feel. She can't understand how this could have happened. They were expecting me in New York *next* Monday. She thought that was understood.

In Edvard Munch's painting *The Scream*, a solitary, empty-eyed figure stands in a roadway clutching its head, mouth open wide. I hope that's not what I look like as I walk the streets of Manhattan during the next several hours, seeing and hearing nothing, waiting for it to be time to return to La Guardia. But it's how I feel. Without making a sound I scream all the way back to Wisconsin.

TODAY IS FRIDAY, the thirteenth of September, the ninety-eighth day of my unemployment. Ninety-nine days ago I was vice president for communications of the J. I. Case Company, a multinational manufacturing corporation with sales of more than five billion dollars a year. Before that I was a vice president at McDonnell Douglas Corporation, a firm that needs no introduction.

And for more than three months now I have been a man with no particular need for an alarm clock, no place where I really need to go in the morning.

This afternoon, to kill a few hours and take my mind off a telephone that will not ring, I played nine holes of golf. For the first time this year it was difficult to find the ball. Small pale leaves are beginning to clutter the fairways, making small white objects hard to see. This is as much reminder as I need of just how long it has been since I last had a job to go to.

On the day I was let go, D day, the sixth of June, the Wisconsin summer was just beginning. I expected—I hoped, anyway—that finding work would take an easy few months, during which I would be free to sleep late, to stay away from neckties for a while, to savor the sweetest part of the northern year.

Now it's fall that is just beginning, and I can see no reason to think that I'm any closer to finding work than I was a season ago. I've had shots at jobs, but every shot has missed. I never got a second chance to meet with Roger Bullard, whose Park Avenue office I visited on the wrong day. Holiday Inns, he told me, has put its search on hold. It's surprising how many searches are supposedly being put on hold these days.

Ninety-eight days. Three months and a week. Not a long time

according to the formula that says a job search is likely to last one month for every ten thousand dollars of annual salary. By this formula, my wait has quite a way to go.

Settle down, I tell myself. Be prepared to keep on waiting as winter moves in. Be prepared to wait through the winter, through another spring, into the summer of next year. And from somewhere inside a voice says faintly that this is easy to say, hard to imagine doing. Getting harder all the time.

I find myself pacing the house at ten in the morning. Though doing it makes me feel like a fool, I find myself reciting a prayer I found in one of those neighborhood-shopper newspapers they give away in supermarkets. It's a prayer to St. Jude, the patron of lost causes. I found it among the classified ads. Somebody had paid to put it there, with an explanatory message. Repeat this prayer seven times daily on nine consecutive days, the message said, and whatever you ask will be granted. At which point you yourself are supposed to pay to run the ad again. "This prayer never fails."

Believe me, I know how ridiculous this is. Even for a believing Catholic this is ridiculous: faith at the level of witches' brew and eye of newt. But I do it all the same, seven times a day—I've got it memorized by now—and when the nine-day cycle comes to an end I start it over again. I ask St. Jude to make some headhunter call and give me the job of my dreams.

Then I recover my senses and tell myself to calm down, stop pacing, find something sensible to do.

I find that I can't do any such thing.

What will I be like by Christmas?

This morning, in the latest of its efforts to jolt the economy to life (I see the economy as a kind of Frankenstein's monster strapped to a table, the Marx brothers at the controls), the Federal Reserve announced a half-point cut in the discount rate. This has happened more times than I can remember in the past three months, and the results are always nil. The economists interviewed on the radio say they expect the results to be nil this time as well. Passing through the kitchen, I make a sour little joke about how happy days are here again. Pam, who quit her own odious job before we knew mine was in danger and now is trying to get herself established in the insurance game, looks up from the table where she's been making her calls. Interest rates went below 2 percent during the Great Depression, she says, and still nothing happened, still nobody would borrow. The government actually succeeded in selling bonds that paid an interest rate of zero.

I keep hearing politicians say that the recession—the Great Recession?—is over. A nice thought, that. But what I see, wherever I look, is more and more good people with good credentials being let go for the first time in their lives and not being able to find work. All I read about is more and more big-name corporations laying off salaried people ten and twenty thousand at a time. I know an amazing number of capable, experienced, college-educated unemployed people. Never in my life, actually, have I seen nearly so many people lose their jobs. And I can't name one who has found a new job. Not one.

Meanwhile, the children of these people are themselves graduating from college and going to work as waitresses and short-order cooks. Class after class piles up one upon another. Some dark part of me is glad about all this: misery does enjoy company. Some other part is trying hard to believe that things really are getting better. That soon I'll be back in a spacious corner office with a secretary bringing me my paper and coffee in a china cup at the start of every day.

Still another part of me is just plain scared. Such a terrible feeling.

The first thing I felt the first time I was fired was surprise—bone-rattling shock at finding myself, for the first time since the week I graduated from grade school, without a place in the world of work. My luck had been so good for so many years that I'd learned to think of it not as luck but as something I had earned, something I was owed. The idea that it could turn bad so abruptly was, for a while, impossible to absorb. I walked the streets in an almost trancelike state, feeling like I was walking on the bottom of the sea, cut off from everything around me and not like other people anymore. I started to daydream about walking through my front door one afternoon and suddenly seeing dozens of people—old bosses, old colleagues, the very people who had done this to me—leap out from behind the furniture and yell "Surprise! Surprise!" In my daydream these people had party hats on. They explained how the whole thing had been part of an experiment of some kind, and how sorry they were to have had to put me through it. Ah well, I say with a smile, all's well that ends well.

It isn't surprising that I was so surprised. Not if you take into account where I started, and where I've been along the way. I began as an urchin, a kid of the streets. Because of the bounty of the American Century (which appears to have lasted a good deal less than fifty years), I ended up with two university degrees plus an extra year as a fellow at Harvard, most of it paid for with other people's money. I started out mopping floors in a decrepit drugstore for fifty cents an hour and went on to jobs of a kind my parents could hardly believe, to an income that passed the furthest limits of my imaginings when I was still in my thirties and kept on climbing from there. I've traveled the world, again mostly on other people's money. I've won semi-high honors, had my picture in the papers, floated above the fields of Normandy in a hot-air balloon.

And now, suddenly, I call it a good day if someone will take my phone call or answer my letter.

Surprise, surprise. I've grown accustomed to surprise.

Resentment too: *Who the hell do these people think they are?* I resent the outplacement people who have been paid big sums (but not of my money, thank God) to help me find a job and appear to be good for nearly nothing. I resent the headhunters, the worst of whom make the outplacement people seem almost noble by comparison.

Above all, I resent the people who put me here, who in the process of making a mess of my life have made a mess of Pam's as well and have left our three children without a place they can think of as home. For twenty years we lived in an old house in a tree-rich old town outside St. Louis. During those years my jobs somehow kept getting better and better, at times almost in spite of me. When Pam entered the world of work, she too did surprisingly well. I expected things to go on in pretty much the same way pretty much forever. I expected to die in that old town eventually; with luck, in that same old house. Where work was concerned, where life was concerned, I'd had more than I'd expected and everything I really wanted.

Eric, a law student now, is the only one of us still in Missouri. Ellen is in graduate school in Minnesota, with no idea where she should go after that. Sarah is in college in Wisconsin, but though Pam and I are in Wisconsin with her, it doesn't seem likely that we'll be here long. When Sarah graduates, where will she go? Wherever Pam and I end up, it's not likely ever to be home to Sarah. Or to Eric, or to Ellen. They don't have a home anymore. Neither, really, do Pam and I. Not in the ways that matter most to us. What we have is a nice house in a town where we haven't lived long and aren't likely to live much longer.

Resentment isn't a strong enough word for what I feel when I think about all this. What do you call resentment when it turns murderous? What's the word for what you're feeling when you daydream about killing people and decide that, no, killing isn't the answer because killing would be too good for them. Killing wouldn't leave *them* in this kind of pain.

There's fear too. It frightens me to see the kinds of corporations that used to hire people like me eliminating more and more of the kinds of jobs that people like me used to have. I'm afraid of what's going to happen to me, to Pam, to all of us.

The fact that I'm fifty years old scares the hell out of me. Not long ago I went to a seminar, supposedly about the subtleties of getting back into the workforce in today's strange job market. In some oblique way, in the midst of a discussion that bounced as aimlessly as a beach ball among fifteen or twenty of us out-of-work "executives," the age question came up. Somebody said that if you run into flagrant age discrimination you can always go to court. *Sure,* somebody else answered. Sure you can—if you're prepared to accept the certainty of never working again. File an age-discrimination complaint the day you win the lottery, somebody said. We all laughed, some nervously, some bitterly.

How the hell can *age* be a factor in my situation? I barely feel grown-up, never mind over-the-hill. I still don't know what I want to be when I do grow up. I can run ten miles in the morning and play tennis the same afternoon. If I need to, I can work twenty hours a day for a week. *Age?* I look in the paper and see that Warren Beatty is starting a family. Not only is he older than I am, he's older by several years. I turn on the tube and see that Senator Bob Dole is still talked about as a possible candidate for president. Bob Dole could be my father. *Age?* Is it really possible?

Envy. I'm jealous of anybody who still has the kind of job I used to have. More and more, I envy almost anybody who still has a job, period. My envy of the people who put me here and are still drawing their giant salaries and piling up their gigantic pension points is as murderous as my resentment.

I envy people who took fewer chances than I did and are now in the safe if charmless harbors that I set sail from years ago: the post office, the Navy, reporting jobs at daily papers. I also envy people who took more chances than I and broke free of salaries and corporations and bullshit. I spend a lot of time wondering where I might be today if I had taken more chances.

If envy caused cancer I'd be dead by Sunday.

Two last things: self-pity and shame. I know that not 1 percent of the human beings now alive in the United States of America, not one tenth of 1 percent of the current inhabitants of Planet Earth, could possibly find me an object worthy of pity. I know too that that's as it should be: imagine feeling sorry for a man whose situation is so tragic that it causes him to play golf on Fridays. Imagine feeling sorry for somebody who is still drawing full pay ninety-eight days after being fired and still has months of full pay ahead of him whether he gets out of bed or not.

And yet I feel sorry for myself constantly. And I want everybody I know to feel sorry for me.

Katharine Hepburn has just published an autobiography in which she offers strong advice: "Don't give in. Fight for your future. Independence is the only solution. Don't moan. Don't complain. Think positively." When I come upon these words in a review I find them inspiring. I actually think, for a moment, of cutting them out and putting them in my wallet. A moment later they look as ridiculous as the idea that the right prayer, said seven times on nine consecutive days, will work a magic spell. Could anything be more ridiculous than talk from a woman born rich and beautiful, a woman who won the first of her four Oscars at age twenty-six and has had all the high-priced work she could handle through the two generations since then? Who never raised a family and never had to wonder if it would be irresponsible to buy a new pair of shoes?

Yes. One thing is more ridiculous. It's more ridiculous for someone like me to start judging a woman I know only from the movies.

Still, sermonettes like hers aren't helpful. I *want* to moan. I want to moan and complain and have somebody hold my head and tell me that everything is going to be all right. I want whoever is doing the telling to make me believe it. Then I want everything actually to be all right.

And if that's not possible I want people to feel sorry for me.

As for shame . . .

I'm ashamed in two ways. On a simple level I'm ashamed of myself for being out of work, for getting my family into such a fix, for allowing myself to become an "executive" in the first place and then letting the whole thing go so wrong. I'm ashamed of myself for losing. When I hear the guy next door start his car in the morning and drive away, I'm ashamed to still be in bed. I'm ashamed to rake leaves on weekday afternoons because everybody in the neighborhood will see—as if they didn't already know—that I don't have an office to go to anymore.

The other shame is deeper and, I think, more important. It has nothing to do with how people see me, everything to do with who I am. In some ways this second shame comes perilously close to self-loathing.

Ask yourself: how are we supposed to react when bad things happen? Everybody knows the answer. The good and the strong react calmly, cheerfully, confidently, bravely. Exactly like Katharine

Hepburn, for all I know. If the good and the strong feel twinges or envy or resentment or fear, they somehow shake such feelings off—dissolving them metabolically, perhaps. Certainly there's no self-pity in such people, no shame, because there's nothing inside they need to be ashamed of.

So. What's wrong with me?

Like a lot of people—like Aristotle, for that matter—I believe that how we're supposed to live our lives is the biggest question of all. And that the old answers to the biggest questions, the answers rooted in the old beliefs, more often than not turn out to be the only answers that work. And that turning to the old answers is usually the best way to get ourselves above fear, self-pity, envy, and all that.

I also believe that though being a corporate executive is a nice enough thing in its way (along with being sometimes an ugly, sometimes a ludicrous thing), it has nothing to do with the big questions and even less to do with the answers.

I've believed these things for years, supposedly. But here I am, up against the most painful crisis of my life. And though it isn't much of a crisis at all compared with what millions of people face (think of Bosnia, of Haiti, of Somalia), all I'm capable of finding inside myself is fear and self-pity and envy. *That,* at bottom, is what I'm most ashamed of.

What do I *really* want? A job as vice president of Holiday Inns? Not likely.

Are the things I'm doing likely to *get* me what I really want? Not likely.

Then why am I *doing* them? Is the real source of my unhappiness the fact that I'm doing the wrong things?

What *should* I be doing?

How much trouble am I in, really?

What *kind* of trouble am I in?

If I'm washed up, how far might I fall?

How much should I care?

Obviously there's a lot more in play here than the simple question of finding a job.

3

A GUY IN CHICAGO tells me that Booz, Allen & Hamilton, the giant management-consulting firm, has a search on for a senior p.r. exec. He doesn't know who's handling it. I unearth the name of the managing partner in Booz, Allen's Chicago office and send him my résumé and a long cover letter. I send them by fax and by mail. He doesn't answer.

Further digging leads to the discovery that the search isn't being handled by the managing partner after all, but by Booz, Allen's vice chairman, one Cyrus Freidheim. His office also is in Chicago. Again I laboriously compose a letter, trying to make Mr. Freidheim see me as wonderfully talented and experienced, as not at all desperate for a job, as enchanted with the idea of joining an organization as supernaturally wonderful as his. This too goes off both by fax and by mail, and it too receives no answer.

I call Freidheim's office. He's out of town. When I identify myself and describe the things I've been sending, the woman at the other end of the line acknowledges that yes, they've been received. I'd like to find out what if anything is being done with them, but she makes it very clear that she has no interest in further conversation. I run for it.

Eventually I send Freidheim a short note saying that I'll be in Chicago on a given day and can arrange to stop in at his office if he will be free to see me. I say I'll give my note a few days to reach him and then follow up by phone. Soon I'm in a nervous lather about the prospect of having to talk once again with the icy-voiced woman.

Who *are* these people? What *kind* of people are they? There was a time, though now it sometimes seems hard to believe, when

I myself was a busy man. I had dozens of people reporting to me, big and complicated projects to manage, bona fide crises screaming for attention. I had trips to take, a phone that rang twenty or thirty times a day, the whole corporate-executive fantasy. But nobody ever telephoned me without getting a reply of some kind, usually fairly promptly. Nobody ever sent me a letter without getting an answer. Nobody. Not ever. Not even the cranks. Not even the people demanding to talk with me about jobs for which they had no visible qualifications. Was I crazy or what?

Better crazy than arrogant, I'm telling myself. Better crazy than hard-hearted. Better crazy and a big fool than a Cyrus Freidheim. I'm really fulminating here, spewing indignation and rank self-righteousness.

But then the phone rings, and on the line is a man who identifies himself as Dick Kinser in New York. He says he's Cyrus Freidheim's executive recruiter—good old Cyrus! How could I have judged him so harshly?—and that he wants to talk with me about the Booz, Allen job. He has to be in Detroit tomorrow. Can I meet him at the airport there?

But from the moment we find each other at the airport, Kinser is coolly distant. He grows no warmer during a long, meandering conversation in a coffee shop booth. I start worrying about the fact that he didn't discover me—that Booz, Allen told him about me, which means I can never be his trophy, his gift to Cyrus Freidheim.

Will this make him want to put other candidates, ones he himself discovered, ahead of me? Should I have contacted him instead of Freidheim? Of course I should have. But how could I? I didn't even know Freidheim was using a headhunter. Freidheim or his secretary—or the first guy I tried to contact, for that matter—could have told me so. It wasn't my fault that they didn't.

I think these things, but I don't say them. To say them would be to challenge Kinser's ability to judge impartially, his professionalism. Not a subject to be touched.

Kinser asks me to mail a list of references to his office in New York. Then he changes his mind, says I should fax the list. It's unusual, in my experience, to be asked for references this early, before being interviewed by the client. It also surprises me that Kinser wants me to fax them. But that's okay. Maybe it means he's more interested than he seems, even if he'll never be able to claim credit for me. The fact that he seems to be in a hurry to check me out can't be bad news.

In the weeks after Detroit I hear nothing. I check with the people I've used as references. They haven't been called. I've never heard of a candidate not being repaid the costs of a trip made at a headhunter's request, and the cost of my ticket was outrageous because I traveled on such short notice. But I am having trouble getting my money back. I make repeated inquiries by phone, never getting past Kinser's secretary and never getting a straight answer. My letters get no answer. Finally I'm so worried I call Freidheim's office to confirm that Kinser really does represent him.

When an envelope finally arrives with a check but no note inside, I count myself lucky not to be out four hundred bucks. And that's the last I ever hear of or from Richard Kinser or Cyrus Freidheim.

This sort of thing does wonders for the old self-confidence.

4

I THINK I CAN tell you how it will happen, if it's going to happen to you.

The first thing they'll do, when they've made their preparations, is get you out of your office and into some other room with some geek from Human Resources.

"Funny how they call themselves Human Resources," I once heard one friend say to another. "They don't seem to be a resource in any way I can see."

"Resource!" exclaimed the second friend, herself a scarred veteran of years in the corporate trenches. "Resource! Hell, they're not even HUMAN!"

Which HR geek is assigned to put the edge of the ax to the back of your neck will depend upon your rank. If you're a vice president your executioner will be a v.p. also—possibly a senior v.p. If you're a director you'll draw an HR director. Managers are done by managers et cetera on down almost but not quite to the ranks of the blue-collar folks who even today do actual work for a living even in these United States of America.

In all likelihood the room where it happens will be the geek's office. In all likelihood you'll have an appointment to report there at some specific time. Maybe the geek's secretary called you to make the appointment a day or two earlier. Getting the time and place pinned down cleared the way for them to make the final arrangements.

If you have an appointment, you'll think it over and try to persuade yourself that there really isn't any reason to worry. If, like me, you have a job that requires regular contact with the HR Department, you'll remember earlier, similar summonses. You'll recall that they led to nothing more terrible than another dumb-ass make-work assignment.

From the moment you pass through his door the HR geek will appear to be in visible pain and eager for you to see it. He wants you to understand that he too is a human being, a nice guy if also a geek, and that his mother didn't raise him for this kind of thing.

"God," said McDonnell Douglas Corporation's senior vice president for Human Resources ten seconds before he fired me. "God, this is going to be hard." He twisted, literally writhed, in his chair. Then he swung back toward me and quickly got down to his work.

If you're the only one being fired, and if they're firing you because they don't love you anymore, the geek will say something about how "this just isn't working out" or "we've decided that we just have to make a change." Something in that vein—something with lots of "just"s in it, tokens of regret and inevitability.

Maybe you haven't been singled out for execution. Maybe you're just one of many victims in a company that's in mortal danger of bankruptcy and therefore downsizing as fast as it can. Or maybe your company isn't in danger at all but is using the troubles of other companies as an excuse to downsize—to "right-size," as they like to say in such cases. Either way, the geek will tell you earnestly how they've been searching high and low but—dammit, what a shame!—there just doesn't seem to be a place for you in the new structure.

"I'm sorry," the senior vice president of J. I. Case Company told me, raising his shoulders and hands in a childlike gesture of helplessness. "We've checked everywhere. We can't find a spot for you."

He'll tell you what kind of separation package has been prepared for you. The rules on this are simple: the less you need, the more you get. If your annual compensation has been in six digits for years and the first digit isn't a 1 anymore, you can expect full pay and benefits for a year and a half, possibly even longer. Six-figure salaries starting with 1 should be good for about a year, six months at a minimum. If your salary is well short of six figures and you have worries about the mortgage and tuition bills, watch out: you're down in dog-eat-dog territory, where they try to get you out the door with as little money as possible.

I have been among the immensely fortunate in this regard. At J. I. Case, after only two and a half years on the job, I was promised up to a year with full pay and benefits while I looked for a new job. At McDonnell Douglas, where my firing turned as messy as a botched execution, they first tried to give me the minimum and then—when I failed to cooperate—changed direction completely. More about that later.

I know people who hired lawyers to handle the negotiation of their separation packages. It cost them a ton, and the results didn't seem to make the expense worthwhile. My impression—based on limited experience, I admit—is that companies tend to dig in and become stubborn when lawyers enter the picture. Companies appear to regard the hiring of a lawyer as an act of betrayal, though how it's possible to betray a company that has just fired you without cause (and is itself protected by phalanxes of lawyers) is one of those questions about modern American business that have no certain answer.

Anyhow, when the geek has delivered his message and demonstrated the depths of his humanity, he'll get up out of his chair and come around from behind his desk. You'll be drawn up after him by some mysterious force resembling magnetism—you don't know how it's happening, but all of a sudden you're on your feet and moving—and together the two of you will glide out the door and down the hall to some smaller office that you probably never noticed before, where somebody you've never seen is waiting to tell you not to worry, everything is going to be fine.

Sometimes other people are waiting in other little rooms nearby, but if you behave yourself you'll never know about them. There might be a company lawyer, for example. You won't see him unless you say something to the HR geek that indicates a less than perfect willingness to be agreeable. If you throw the HR geek off balance, though, he'll bring the lawyer onstage fast. That happened to me at McDonnell Douglas.

In the more paranoid kinds of company somebody from security might be hidden in the wings, too. You'll see the security guy only if you display truly flagrant disregard for the geek's delicate feelings—by taking his throat in your two hands, for example. I never knew about this until my friend Dave, head of security at J. I. Case, got downsized himself and started telling about the things he'd been expected to do.

The stranger waiting for you in the little office, the one telling you that everything is going to be all right, is the outplacement geek. He's a representative of a new species in American business, newer even than the headhunter. He's been brought in, and will be paid handsomely, to "guide you through your transition." The HR geek will introduce you—handshakes and small, rueful smiles all around—and exit as fast as he can.

Is it flippant of me to call these people "geeks"? Originally the word referred to individuals who did revolting things for money at carnivals and fairs. Someone paid to bite the heads off live chickens and snakes—that was a geek. I don't think I'm being flippant at all.

The outplacement geek assigned to your case will direct you into a chair. He'll be the nicest of nice guys—one of the main reasons he was called to his profession in the first place. He'll give you another small, slightly rueful smile. He'll say that he understands what a shock this is but that he also knows something important: that it's very likely the start of a better life not just for you but for your whole family. If he was ever fired himself (many outplacement geeks are former victims), he'll tell you about it, encouraging you to appreciate how beautifully *that* worked out in the end. If his autobiography doesn't fit he'll tell you about one or two of his past clients—how one of them is now King of Samoa and the other is expected to be nominated for the Nobel Prize next week. He'll ask whether everything will be okay at home, whether you expect to have trouble telling your spouse about all this. When you say no he'll give you his card and urge you to take things easy for a day or two but then to come see him at his office.

"I know it can be hard to believe at a time like this," my first outplacement geek actually told me, "but it really is true that this could turn out to be the best thing that ever happened to you."

The outplacement geek also wants to think of himself as a useful citizen. As a kind of midwife, not as an accessory after the fact.

Which is understandable, of course. Not many of our mothers had anything like this in mind for us when they brought us into the world.

Not many of us want to do these things we do for pay.

5

A GUY IN Chicago, a friend of a guy I know, tells me that Gerber Products, the outfit that makes baby food, has a search on.

I look up Gerber in Standard & Poor's *Register of Corporations, Directors, and Executives*. Gerber is based in Michigan, and its vice president for Human Resources is named Curtis Mairs. I wait until just after six and try to call Mairs. Calling very early or very late in the day is a good tactic: the secretaries are usually off duty then, so that even senior executives are sometimes left unprotected. And today it works: Mairs picks up his own phone, and he doesn't hang up as I hurriedly introduce myself. I say I've heard he's looking for a p.r. exec. Not wanting to repeat what may have been my big mistake with Booz, Allen, I say I'd like the name of the recruiter handling the search.

"You might try Steven Seiden," he says. "In New York." He hangs up.

There's a New York listing for Seiden Associates, Inc., in my *Directory of Executive Recruiters*. And it is indeed headed by a Steven Seiden. I spend much of the evening writing and rewriting a letter.

I try to show Seiden how right I would be for Gerber Products: "My hope is to associate myself with a solid company with a genuine desire for first-rate performance across the whole communications spectrum . . . "

And the splendor of my qualifications: "I have a solid and consistent record of success," et cetera, et cetera.

First thing the next morning I call Seiden's office and get his fax number. Then I drive to the EconoPrint shop and have my letter and my résumé transmitted. Next I put the letter and the résumé into a manila envelope, drive to the post office, and send them off by Priority Mail.

The next night Seiden calls. Bingo. We talk for a long time. He goes through my résumé line by line, asking for details about everything.

"Well," he says at a point where he appears to have run out of questions. "Well, all of it sounds pretty impressive. On the face of it. As far as it goes."

That sounds so strange. *On the face of it?* Does he think I'm pretending to be somebody I'm not?

He asks something I haven't been asked before: he wants me to describe my appearance. When I do so, fumblingly, he asks how tall I am. How much I weigh. Whether I have a beard. A mustache. He asks me to send a photo of myself.

What?

We agree that I will also send him samples of my work. Overeager as usual, I say I can send it by Express Mail if that will help. I point out that Express Mail is the only possible way of getting anything to him before the end of the week. He says that will be helpful indeed.

Once again I sit up late composing a letter intended to make me seem brilliant and clever, motivated but not *desperate.* You never want to seem desperate. When I'm satisfied with the letter's tone I print it out and put it into an envelope on top of a fat stack of supporting evidence: corporate annual reports, articles and speeches, official descriptions of my last two jobs, charts of departments I've headed, a survey showing that business editors rated one of those departments among the best in the country after I'd been running it for seven years . . .

Fat yellow envelope in hand, I'm at the post office when it opens in the morning.

Seiden calls again early the following week. He says he's received my envelope, has examined most of the contents, and finds it "very impressive—assuming it all checks out."

Again: strange. Does he think I've forged this stuff?

Days later I arrive home to find a message saying that Seiden has called and wants me to call him back. When I give my name to the woman who answers his phone she puts me through. The man on other end of the line is a new Seiden. I've never heard him so positive.

"Listen, I'm in a meeting and can't talk now," he says. "But I want you to know that I really am interested in you for the Gerber thing. I'll be back to you soon. This search is *"not*–the italics are in his voice–going to go ahead without you in it. I'll be back to you soon–in hours, not days. You'll hear from me again in *hours, not days.*"

Wow. Hot to trot. Could the stuff I mailed him have caused this sudden and profuse flowering of enthusiasm? I get my atlas and start looking for Gerber's hometown, Fremont, on the map of Michigan. It's way out in the sticks. But near what I've been told is the best steelhead fishing in North America. Can't be all bad.

Taking Seiden at his word, I begin to watch the clock. The day ends without another call. The next days end the same way, and so does the week. Despite what he said, clearly Seiden is operating on a basis of days, not hours. Then it's weeks, not days. After a very long time I try to call him, don't get through, leave my name and number.

More than a week after that Pam and I arrive at home one Sunday night and find a message on the machine. The voice of Steven Seiden says, in a bored way, that he's returning my call.

Returning my call? Which call? The one from the week before last?

He has left his home number but cautioned me not to disturb him after ten-thirty New York time. It's precisely ten-thirty in New York when I hear the message. After a moment of agonizing I decide not to call back then.

The next morning I call his office, leave a message, get nothing back. In the evening I call him at home. His wife answers and says in a cheery voice that he's gone out briefly but will call me back soon.

He doesn't. He never calls again. Eventually, many weeks later, an envelope arrives from his office. In it is a copy of the news release announcing that a new vice president of communications has been appointed at the Gerber Products Company.

The winner is from Chicago. I recognize his name. He's the guy who told me about the Gerber search in the first place.

Small world.

6

POSITIVE THINKING is what I need. Everybody says so. Norman Vincent Peale made a career out of saying so, Katharine Hepburn says so today. So do all the people peddling books and videos and seminars about how really really *really* wanting something can make it come to pass.

I don't know what to think about positive thinking. Sometimes, for brief moments, I believe in it. I watch some motivational speaker, Les Brown or one of the others, shouting and sweating and walking back and forth onstage telling stories about people who believed they could work miracles and went out and worked them. When I'm listening to these stories they make sense. *Yeah,* I say to myself. *That's right.* I begin to think that I've known people who have done such things. That I can do them myself.

Then the show is over and my blood cools. I go back to my usual way of thinking, back to the thought that all this hot talk falsifies things, that it denies at least half of life's big truths. It denies the tragic dimension, the one in which people *really* want something and *really* try hard to achieve what they want and are broken in the process.

Doesn't life break everybody in the end?

Anyway, positive thoughts are definitely what I need right now. Positive "outcomes," as they say on mahogany row. The mythology of American business won't be satisfied unless and until the mess I'm in turns out to be the best thing that ever happened to me.

Everybody knows how the story goes. "We had to get rid of old Charlie, and at first he was pretty bitter. But in the end he got another job that he liked much better. And the new job pays more than the old one, and it's given him a whole new lease on life. It turned out to be *the best thing that ever happened to him."* Telling the story, hearing it, makes everybody feel better. Too bad it's so hard to believe these days. Too bad real-life examples have become so hard to find.

I don't need this to turn out to be the best thing that ever happened to me. I'll be satisfied, I'll be grateful, if it turns out to be something less than a disaster. If it ends with me in a new job that's more than barely tolerable, with my life not totally deranged and Pam and the kids not permanently hurt. If it ends that way I will, so help me, get down on my knees in gratitude.

What I keep thinking about, though, is not exciting new opportunities or the delights that are still to come.

What I think about is Bobby Joyce.*

Bobby Joyce lived in my neighborhood when I was a kid and was a year ahead of me at St. Mark's grade school and later at McBride High. He was a big, good-looking Irishman of the black-haired, white-skinned Snow White type, cocky, arrogant, unfailingly sarcastic, athletically brilliant. He was the kind who only had time for the people he thought were okay, and he didn't think many people were okay. I can see today that so much lip-curling contempt must have been a mask for some kind of hurt, but at the time it didn't seem at all strange because to my eyes it wasn't at all unwarranted. Bobby Joyce was the epitome of cool.

When I picture him I always see him chewing gum and smiling a kiss-my-ass Elvis-like sarcastic smile out of the corner of his mouth. *Cool.* He showed us how it was possible to be smart-ass cool even in a cassock and surplice. Even up on the altar, serving Mass. I'm sure he didn't chew gum while serving Mass, but it isn't hard to picture him that way.

Thirty years out of high school, I found myself seated next to another St. Mark's old-timer, Jimmy Monahan, at some sort of downtown business lunch. Jimmy had been a few years ahead of

---

* *A pseudonym.*

Bobby Joyce in school, which put him several years ahead of me. He'd always been the friendly sort, though, even to us little guys. He was in the seminary for a while after high school, then in law school for a while. When I ran into him he was the advertising manager for an insurance company. He had the creased face and tired, unjudging eyes of a decent man for whom life has not been a picnic. As the luncheon broke up and we were moving toward the door he somehow mentioned the Joyce brothers—something about how miserable it was, what had happened to them.

I couldn't let it go; I had to ask. Bobby's older brother, Len, had died of cancer, Jimmy said. Bobby himself had become an accountant—maybe just a bookkeeper, I'm not sure—and spent decades with some company before losing his job.

After a year of failing to find a new job, Jimmy said tiredly, Bobby killed himself. He did it by throwing himself off the Union Avenue viaduct onto some old railroad tracks at the northern edge of the neighborhood where we'd all been schoolboys together.

I don't know what season it happened in. I don't know if he was unshaven and wearing a tattered McBride letterman's jacket or his last good suit or what. But in my mind's eye I see it happening on a raw winter's day, a black-and-white turned-up-collars day like some scene from *On the Waterfront*. It's hard to draw a connection between the beautiful boy I remember and the spent man I see pulling himself up onto the viaduct's concrete railing and getting ready to step off.

Right there you have the polar extremes of this situation.

On your left, ladies and gentlemen, the best thing that ever happened to me.

On your right, a hard kind of death in an empty railroad yard.

Bobby Joyce, uncrowned king of the kids, dead of a year without work.

There is no overstating how eager I am for this to turn out to be the best thing that ever happened to me. There are few things I'm not willing to do to make that happen.

But what I keep thinking of is Bobby Joyce.

7

If OUTPLACEMENT resembles anything, it's probably most like Purgatory. You don't want to be there, you wouldn't be there if you'd been better or smarter or luckier, and the only point in being there is doing what you can to get out.

There's one big difference, though. In Purgatory, if I have the story straight, you're certain to move up eventually. Outplacement is a Purgatory in which you might move up—could conceivably make the greatest leap of your life—but also might still go to Hell. Purgatory must, in some way, be a place of hope, if not of joy. It's true that there's hope in outplacement, but there's also a whole lot of fear. And ample room for despair. Especially in times like these.

"I don't know what I can tell you," I said to my daughter Ellen after I'd been fired by J. I. Case and had been in outplacement a month. We were talking about her plans for graduate school, and how much help she could expect from home. "A year from now I might be inviting you to come join us in the Riviera. A year from now I might be completely up the creek. Anything could happen, and there's no way of knowing what will."

I think we can now rule out one of those extremes. I'm not likely to be inviting anybody to the Riviera.

Showing up at your assigned outplacement office for the first time is a lot like my idea of arriving in Purgatory. For one thing there's the sheer brutal shock of it, the difficulty of believing that you really are dead—really are out of work.

"This can't be happening! Things like this don't happen to ME!"

Then there's the discovery that being dead isn't as remarkable as you'd thought. The first time I was ever in an outplacement office was the day after I'd been fired for the first time. The man assigned to be my counselor was showing me around, explaining the system, all but chucking me under the chin to brighten my spirits. I was still stunned, numb, not at all interested in being cheered up.

He showed me rows of cubicles where former low-level managers were talking quietly into telephones. He showed me corridors lined with little offices—wooden doors, walls that went all the way to the ceiling—where former middle managers also were talking on phones. Finally he showed me a more spacious, more handsomely furnished office. It was unoccupied. It was going to be mine, he said. Because of my rank. Because I was a displaced officer of mighty McDonnell Douglas.

That was supposed to make me feel better, I guess. In fact, it made me feel terrible. It made me feel painfully different from all the men and women in the cubicles and in the little offices. It made me think that it must be a rare and truly terrible thing for someone to fall as far as I had just fallen.

But then my guide led me into the "library," a near-to-bookless kind of conference room where several men in neckties were bending over copies of *The Wall Street Journal* and *The National Employment Weekly*. And immediately I realized that I was looking into the faces of two people I'd known at McDonnell Douglas. Not former officers, but pretty senior executives all the same.

"Hey!" I said, suddenly and indecently elated. "I didn't know you were fired too!" Purgatory could easily be a lot like this. It's easy to imagine being newly dead but breaking into a big smile and saying "Hey, I didn't know you were dead too!"

I wasn't in outplacement long that first time—just one day. But this time I've been there for months, with no escape in sight. And there hasn't been a week when new crops of people I used to know at J. I. Case haven't shown up, freshly fired, along with a lot of people from other companies as well. It's a bloodbath out there, part of the national massacre I learn more about every time I pick up a paper. Whenever I see a newly arrived familiar face there's an abrupt outbreak of good humor and cries of "Hey . . ."

Hey . . . so you're dead too, are you?

I always ask the newcomers from Case for news about the office, and they tell me tales out of Hunter S. Thompson, tales of fear and loathing. They ask me about outplacement. When nobody else is around they ask whether the staff, the counselors, can be trusted. I give them the basic rule: don't let the counselors overhear anything you wouldn't want to get back to the people paying the bills, the people who fired you, the people who could cut off your separation pay. We're like characters in some George Raft prison movie, talking about the screws. We trade stories about who's been in Purgatory for a year already and seems no closer to deliverance than when he began. We tell stories, if we have any, about the ones who have gone on to Paradise.

When you find yourself in outplacement it's because your former employers have paid to get you in. The price of admission is not trivial: a month and a half of your salary is pretty much the standard. What you get for this is working space with desk and phone, access to a pot of coffee, the use of a clerical staff and various office equipment and a pitiful excuse for a library. You share in the services of a receptionist who answers the phone by saying "executive offices" *(wouldn't it be fun if just once she said "Purgatory"?)* and takes any messages you're lucky enough to get. For what it's worth—not necessarily a great deal—you get the advice and the pep talks of your assigned counselor.

Some outplacement firms offer psychological testing, free of charge. What the hell, I said to myself when I was told about this. Why not?

So arrangements were made for me to visit a local shrink. He turned out to be a clean-cut, agreeable, earnest young man who might have passed for a golf pro or second vice president of the Indianapolis Jaycees. He asked me questions about my life and the jobs I'd had, the things that had happened to me, how I felt about all of it. I answered as honestly as I could—why not? What was he going to do if he didn't like my answers? Turn me over to the neurosis patrol?

After the interview he gave me a long written test, one of those preference things they give in high school. Would you rather eat a carrot or go for a ride in a bus? Mow the grass or wash the dog?

A week later I went back for the results. The psychologist told me that although I appeared to understand the politics of corporate life well enough, I was probably not very good at playing them. I had no argument with that.

He said I ought to think twice before taking another job in manufacturing. That made sense to me.

That it had probably been a mistake for me to get involved with manufacturing companies in the first place.

That the kinds of people who run American manufacturing companies are incapable of understanding people like me.

And that I'm the kind of person who has great difficulty understanding them.

What the hell, I said to myself. Where was this guy when I really needed him? When I still had options?

You can go to outplacement every day, or every other day, or once a week, or once a month. It depends on how determined you are, or how futile the whole thing has started to seem. If it does nothing else, outplacement can give you a reason to put on a white shirt and tie and get into your car in the morning. By doing that it saves you from never getting out of your pajamas and slowly descending into a vegetative state.

Outplacement will also assist you in the mechanics of a job search. The counselors at outplacement are inclined to make a huge, complicated, weeks-long negotiation process out of the essentially quite simple task of putting together your résumé. It's something for them to *do*, I suspect. Laboriously, with much faux profundity, they will tell you how to prepare a letter to go with your résumé. Little that they say in this connection is not known already to anyone with a modicum of knowledge of life and of business.

They will show you how to assemble a mailing list using the *Directory of Executive Recruiters* and directories of corporations and directories of far more things than you ever thought anyone would want to make directories of. They will talk about networking and tell you that if you're serious about getting out of Purgatory you're going to have to telephone everybody you know—and a great many people you don't know.

"Mr. Johnson? Mr. Johnson, my name is Jerry Meyer. I'm the communications vice president at the J. I. Case Company here in Wisconsin. Joe Smith at Consolidated Amalgamated gave me your name. About a week ago I sent you a letter that I hope has reached you by now. As my letter indicated, I've reached a point in my career where I'm interested in exploring some new options"—am I ever—"and I'm wondering if you've heard of any searches it might be worthwhile for me to check out."

Calls of this kind are most productive when made to people who occupy jobs you'd like to have. It's wise to call such people because they're the people the headhunters call when looking for someone like you. And because they're the people most likely to know other people exactly like themselves—and like you. They're your professional peer group, the national network for your line of work, the great transcontinental grapevine.

The importance of the peer group cannot be overestimated. This is the main reason why there are so many professional associations in this country. And why those associations have so many meetings and so many committees and subcommittees that also meet often. And why so many people eagerly go to those meetings (at their employers' expense, of course). They go to start weaving together the network they're going to need when they get into trouble.

When someone you call gives you a lead, you offer profuse thanks and follow up with a letter that repeats those thanks even more profusely. When someone talks with you but doesn't give you a lead you thank him anyway, leave your name and number, ask to be remembered the next time a lead turns up. You send a letter that says, thanks again for talking with me, I sure hope you'll keep me in mind.

That, in a nutshell, is how networking is done in Purgatory. It's far from rocket science, but when done on a big enough scale it's unfailingly productive. Doing it on a big enough scale, of course, takes an immense amount of time. Thus the one indisputably true saying of the outplacement counselors: looking for a job is a full-time job.

Dave, who used to be the head of security at J. I. Case and has become my best friend in outplacement, somehow got a copy of a directory of all the corporate security chiefs in America. Every day, hour after hour, he goes through his directory page by page, entry by entry, dialing and talking, dialing and talking, gradually accumulating leads like a prospector panning gold nuggets out of a gravel creek bed. The key, says Dave, is never letting anybody know that you're not still working. "Everybody out there is scared these days," says Dave. "Everybody is looking for contacts that might be helpful sooner or later. If they think you're actually working, they'll think of you as a future contact. They take your call, and they usually seem willing to tell you what they know. They try to help in the hope that some day you'll help them back."

Dave's leads, unfortunately, have not yet led to a single interview. The problem, I guess, is that he's well past fifty. But he never gives up, and though he makes a lot of sour jokes he never complains. He never even slows down. Thanks to a late second marriage, he has two kids under age ten. I worry about him, and I admire his grit. I wish him success almost as much as I wish myself success.

Dave's experience, by the way, also confirms my skepticism about the value of lawyers in getting the best separation package for yourself. Because he wasn't a vice president, Dave got a meager package from J. I. Case. He paid a lawyer to write a letter asking for a few extra months of pay, and the company never responded. So Dave finally asked directly, and they gave him what he asked.

If you're in outplacement and you know what's good for you, you force yourself—positive thinking, remember—to be as much like Dave as you can. You listen attentively to the counselors as they tell miracle stories about people just like you who wrote and wrote and called and called and got absolutely nowhere until one day—wonder of wonders—the jobs of their dreams fell swooning into their arms. Above all, you force yourself to dig deeper and deeper into the directories and dredge up more and more names. There are hundreds of headhunter firms in the U.S. today, many thousands of individual headhunters. And one of the rules of outplacement says that if you haven't sent your résumé to some particular headhunter within the past six months, it's time to do so again. If you send out a thousand résumés in June and are still out of work in December, do it again. There's enough work in this to keep any-body busy for a lifetime.

As for whether it actually makes sense, is actually going to pay off . . .

What *else* are you going to do?

So you pick up that phone and you *force* yourself to make those calls.

But unless you're luckier than most or the job market gets a lot better than it's been lately, you'll discover that it's possible to send off five hundred résumés with five hundred customized cover letters and not get a single reply more substantial than a preprinted postcard saying thanks.

You'll learn that after a while it can become very hard to think of new people to call, harder still to call the same people for the third or the fourth time.

You'll find that gradually some of your fellow deceased aren't showing up at their cubicles very often anymore. Some of them will drift away completely, and you'll remember their dark jokes about becoming a security guard or moving north to where somebody's son-in-law knows about a job driving a delivery truck. You'll wonder what happened to them but not want to call and find out.

Once in a while somebody will land a job and bring in a box of doughnuts to celebrate, but that won't happen nearly as often as anyone would like. When it does happen you'll find it awk-wardly hard to seem joyous. Meanwhile, new people will keep showing up, and the place will get so crowded you'll have to call ahead in the morning and reserve the use of a cubicle.

You'll see how every week a little more confidence has drained out of the eyes of the people who keep coming back, so that after a while they look as if they're afraid of life.

You'll reflect that exactly the same change must be taking place in your eyes. You'll want to stay home and never get out of your pajamas. But you won't dare.

And what you thought was Purgatory will start to look a lot like Hell.

8

IT WAS *such* a good gig.

I think those are the saddest words I ever heard Pam say. She said them shortly after I was fired/ for the first time. They are buried in my breast like an arrowhead.

Pam and I were stupidly young when we got married. I was just out of grad school and waiting to enter the Navy and didn't even have a job. I also didn't have any money. Pam had finished two years of college and had a lot of solid experience as a waitress.

Our first house, when we bought it four years later with two thousand dollars down, was so small that we went out looking for extra-small furniture. She paid for the carpet and a sofa bed by working evenings for a while as a typist in the office of a motorcycle insurance company. By the time she graduated from college—itself a kind of financial miracle—we had two kids. We had three when she announced that she'd been at home long enough and was going out to work. The first thing that changed when she landed a spot in Washington University's publications office was that suddenly we had room in the budget for all five of us to go out to pizza joints and hamburger restaurants almost every Friday night.

Pam was quick-witted, dazzlingly articulate, a talker and a laugher, somewhere between exceptionally pretty and flat-out beautiful. I was ponderous, silent, straw-haired and heavy-featured, inclined even in the best of times to be a little glum. An odd couple for sure. But there was commitment on both sides and we made it work.

Pam never expected much and never cared much about impressing people. When I decided to leave newspaper reporting for public relations, she tried to talk me out of it. She said it was wrong for me—that I was born to write for newspapers. The first time we moved to a bigger house, she went along with the idea reluctantly. The second time, I almost had to wrestle her to the ground to get her to agree.

Then came ten years when everything fell into our laps. Everything. In its coverage of a super-fancy shindig at which Luciano Pavarotti sang, the *St. Louis Post-Dispatch* reported the presence of "the glamorous-looking Pam and Jerry Meyer." We laughed about what we were going to have to do to get promoted from "glamorous-looking" to "glamorous."

And then the chairman of McDonnell Douglas Corporation retired, and for us the golden years came to an end. Before very long, left naked to my enemies, I was thrown out. It became clear that if I were going to get another job anything like the job I'd lost, it would have to be in another city. Which meant that Pam, too, would have to leave her job and try to get another elsewhere. Which meant good-bye to house, good-bye to friends, good-bye to so many things we treasured that the mere thought of leaving was like tearing out an internal organ with our bare hands.

In the process of absorbing what was happening, we talked a lot, talked obsessively, about how unbelievable the whole thing was. And about how at the same time it wasn't even unusual in today's corporate world. About how lucky we were to have had so many great years. And about how, one way or another, it was sure to work out in the end.

After all, it always had. Our son Eric had been born with a complete bilateral cleft lip and palate. The doctors couldn't tell us whether he'd ever be able to speak. In high school he won the Outstanding Speaker award three years running and was state champion in the Voice of Democracy contest. In college he got lead roles in plays.

One day Pam said again how lucky we were. I felt that way too. Deep down, I'd never really believed it could continue.

"I guess it was just too good to last," she said slowly.

Then, after a long contemplative pause: "But it was *such* a good gig while it lasted."

Regret—grief—was so thick in the air I could barely see her through it.

Now it's happened again. Another hard fall, and before the injuries from the first have had a good chance to heal.

Pam is the queen of the good sports. She is a remarkably resilient creature. She doesn't complain, she certainly doesn't blame, but I know she's hurting at least as much as I am.

9

I LEARN FROM a friend of a friend in Chicago (networking bingo) that a company I've never heard of, an outfit called Imcera Group, has a search on for a vice president of public relations. Immediately I send my résumé to the headhunter handling the search.

Just a few days later the headhunter calls to ask me about myself. Bingo.

A few days after that he calls again and invites me to visit him at his office. Bingo bingo.

We talk for two and a half hours. His name is Larry Massé, and he seems an intelligent and decent enough guy. His questions are good, some of them showing surprising insight into the corporate communications game. I drive home thinking that I probably did okay, though I'm not entirely sure.

In less than a week, arrangements are made for me to meet at Imcera Group's headquarters with the company's HR v.p., who turns out to be a big, bricklike woman with the bearing of a sergeant of military police. She puts me on a sofa in her office and for almost two hours does her best to grill me, asking questions that oscillate back and forth between banality and meaninglessness. In the end, smiling, she tells me she wants me to come back for a visit with the company's soon-to-retire chief executive and the man who's been chosen to succeed him.

When I report the good news to the outplacement staff, I'm told that this is a very big bingo, that when you're interviewing at the CEO level you're definitely in the running. For this kind of assessment they get paid?

In the midst of all the bingos, I'm starting to find myself interested in Imcera Group. At not much more than a billion dollars, its annual sales make it smaller than any corporation I've ever worked for. But now I know that its offices are quietly elegant, and though I don't think this ought to impress me, the truth is that it does. Now I know too that Imcera Group is an admirably efficient little moneymaker, getting remarkably good returns from the manufacture of pharmaceuticals for animals and an assortment of other things having to do with chemicals. Financial analysts say they expect it to do even better over the next ten years. Consistent profits suggest job security—no small attraction after my experience at J. I. Case.

Imcera Group does much of its business overseas and plans to do more; I enjoy the international stuff. Imcera Group's two largest divisions are based in St. Louis; my elderly parents, my son and his bride-to-be, my sister and her husband and kids, most of my other relatives, and most of the friends I have in the world all live in St. Louis.

In making arrangements for my meetings with the two big guys, both Larry Massé and the HR woman tell me that I'll find them very different from each other. They describe the retiring CEO, George Kennedy, as a brilliant personality, a phenomenon. Subtly, they give me to understand that Kennedy's anointed heir, one Dr. M. Blakeman Ingle, though of course impressive beyond human powers of description (what man or woman who reported to him could possibly say otherwise?), is less polished, less sure of himself, less easy to know.

Thus I prepare myself for a memorably fun visit with the delightful Mr. Kennedy, prepare to be patient and understanding where poor Dr. Ingle is concerned.

I arrive early at the suburban office park where Imcera Group has its offices. Half an hour after the appointed time I'm still idling in the lobby. When Kennedy's secretary finally leads me into his office, he isn't there. She invites me to make myself comfortable. When instead of sitting down I cross the room to inspect his bookcases she says, in a voice lightly tinctured with affection and pride, that "Yes, he's quite the reader." A bookworm myself, I see an opportunity in this, the chance that some shared interest might provide material for the icebreaking part of our talk. I scan the shelves, searching for something I know and can say something about.

No such luck. All the books here are recent best-sellers, either spy novels and thrillers or the latest popular nostrums about how to succeed in business by following some simple formula. Airport books. In two big bookcases I can't find a single volume that brings an interesting question to mind. I take the cup of coffee the secretary has offered me and find myself a chair.

When he arrives, Kennedy seems distracted, harried, uninterested. He's a big man, white-haired and craggy-faced, and he seems almost annoyed by my presence, trying without trying very hard to conceal his annoyance, not caring a bit that he isn't succeeding. Dropping into the big chair behind his big bare desk, he looks at his watch and says something about an airplane. He tosses me a question so broad, so obviously a pro forma time-killer—"So tell me why you're here?" "What can I do for you?" something like that—that for a panicky instant my mind goes blank. I draw myself forward in my seat, try to remember to look friendly and relaxed and eager, and start talking about what I know of Imcera Group and about my own background and how it seems possible that the two might fit together. He glances out the window, tosses me another empty question, and we go on from there.

At one point, apropos of I don't know what, Kennedy says that in his opinion Imcera Group's new communications vice president will have to be one thing above all: an excellent writer. This surprises me—neither the headhunter nor the HR woman has even mentioned writing—but it gives me an opportunity to talk about the writing I've done. If any of this impresses Kennedy, if any of it even interests him, he must be unbeatable at poker. We go on this way for fifteen, perhaps twenty minutes. I answer his content-free questions with one part of my brain while trying, with some other part, to come up with an interesting question or two to ask when my turn comes.

My turn never comes. Suddenly Kennedy is on his feet and looking at his watch again and maneuvering me toward the door.

He leads me back to the lobby, disconnecting himself from me when we get to the sofa where I'd been waiting earlier. Pointing to his watch, he says something to the receptionist about O'Hare. Then, with a vague wave of his hand, he disappears in the direction of the parking lot.

This has been about as unsatisfactory an interview as I could imagine short of something ending in fisticuffs. I try to reassure myself, noting that Kennedy is, after all, about to retire. Probably he has very little interest in the selection of a new vice president. Probably I was sent to see him simply as a courtesy, so that he wouldn't feel ignored. And the man does have a plane to catch.

I pin my hopes on Dr. M. Blakeman Ingle.

IO

My MEETING with Dr. M. Blakeman Ingle–"Blake," he says as he offers his hand–turns out to be as unexpectedly good as the interview with Kennedy had been unexpectedly awful. Ingle, I know from checking, started his career as a research scientist and moved into general management relatively late. And he is indeed, as I'd been warned, the furthest thing from charismatic. He's short and chubby, like somebody's dough-faced, soft-spoken, slightly frumpy uncle. Instead of withdrawing behind his desk, he seats us together at a coffee table, and as we talk I begin to get the impression that here is an intelligent, thoughtful, good-humored, unpretentious man. Here is an executive who actually appears to be paying attention to the things I am saying. Here is someone in whose company it might be possible to earn a living while still functioning as a human being.

I'm with Ingle for nearly an hour and a half, and my good impression of him continues to grow. Early in our meeting he brings up a subject that I'd simultaneously foreseen, dreaded, and hoped for: Have I seen Imcera Group's latest annual report? What do I think of it?

"I'm going to be frank with you," I say, taking a copy of the report out of my briefcase and thumbing it open. "I think there are serious problems with this thing. Serious . . . deficiencies." I'm not really being frank. I don't merely think that the Imcera Group annual has problems. I think it stinks. I think it's about as bad as corporate annual reports ever get, which is saying a great deal indeed. I explain what seems bad to me about the writing (it's pompous and obscure, though I don't use those words), the design (whoever did it must have been delirious), and the presentation of data (incomprehensible). The whole report, I've thought since the first time I looked at it, seems almost purposely designed to—and I do use these words on Ingle—to "deter readership."

It's possible, of course, that Ingle himself is the primary architect of this report. It's possible that everything I dislike about it is a direct reflection of him. If so—if this is his idea of what an annual report should be—there's little likelihood of our working together successfully. As badly as I'm starting to want this job, it seems necessary to be fairly forthright about something so fundamental.

"Well, actually," Ingle responds slowly and softly after what seems a long hesitation, "actually I agree with you." Then, obviously trying to be very diplomatic himself, he gives me to understand that the report is the work of Mr. Kennedy, who regards himself as a master of all things remotely literary or artistic. This fits with things I've been told about Kennedy. I know, for example, he was the genius who came up with "Imcera" as the company's name. He took the initials of a predecessor corporation, International Minerals and Chemicals, and improvised from there, thereby creating a name that no one who reads it knows how to pronounce, that no one who hears it knows how to spell, and that I myself have found damnably hard to remember.

Ingle says that although Kennedy is retiring as CEO he plans to remain as chairman of the board for two years more and is sure to take a strong interest in the company's future reports. Uh-oh. I try to indicate that I've been around long enough to understand such things—to understand the importance of handling them delicately.

The interview continues to go well, and I leave with the feeling that my relatively risky response to the annual report question had worked out fine. That I scored a point or two early in the game and came away with a win.

All that happens on a Tuesday. I spend the next several days thinking about all the ways in which a job with Imcera Group could be good for me, good for all of us. By Friday, having heard nothing, I ring Larry Massé. He takes the call—not something to be taken for granted where headhunters are concerned—and is friendly, encouraging, positive. He sounds (I'm abjectly attentive to the tones of his voice) happy to hear from me.

I say I'm curious about how things stand at Imcera Group.

"The only negative feedback I've had is some feeling that you were a little slow to warm up. During your visit, I mean. I told them I'd talked with you at great length and I felt you'd warmed up just fine. How do you feel about that?"

"About what?"

"About what they said—about you being slow to warm up."

"Well, it makes me feel kinda bad, to be honest about it. I thought our talks were good. I didn't spend much time with Mr. Kennedy, but he was busy and needed to get to O'Hare."

"Hey!" Massé says heartily. "Don't feel bad about it. There's nothing to feel bad *about*. It was just an offhand comment—three points off, at worst, out of a possible hundred. You're still *very* much a candidate. If you still *want* to be."

When I try to find out who found me "slow to warm up," Massé goes vague. After the call, deep in agony, I try to figure it out.

Is it even possible that Kennedy would write me off on the basis of our short, strange, distracted exchange? If Ingle had found me non-warm, I could accept his decision even though I wouldn't understand it. Ingle, at least, gave me a chance. But Kennedy? After seeming interested in nothing but the airport?

Hell, there's no way of knowing whether Kennedy is the problem, or whether it's Ingle, or whether there *is* a problem.

Massé has told me that nothing can possibly happen during the week ahead because Kennedy, Ingle, and the HR woman will all be traveling. I wait through that week as patiently as possible, sending out more résumés, making more calls, reciting the prayer to St. Jude. On Friday it suddenly, urgently occurs to me that I could have sent letters to all three of the Imcera people—and that, therefore, I should have done so. Hurriedly I put together three letters, trying to impress them with how much I like them and their company ("a challenging, stimulating place to work," et cetera), how much I could relish the job they're considering me for ("obviously crucial to the long-term success of the organization," et cetera et cetera), how much I hope there will be opportunities for us to talk further.

I hurry to the mailbox so these letters will be picked up at the end of the day and delivered on Monday.

When Monday comes I read my copies of the letters, trying to see them through the eyes of the recipients. They look perhaps just a little overearnest but basically okay. What the hell—why worry about *that?* The outplacement people are constantly urging me to follow up every telephone conversation with a letter (as well as following up every letter with a phone conversation), and always to be as enthusiastic as possible.

I start hoping for the phone to ring. I think about calling Massé to see what he knows and decide that I've probably called him enough. I swallow increasing amounts of anxiety all day Tuesday, and I get through Wednesday only by promising myself that if I hear nothing by Friday I'll call then. Thursday is hell. Friday morning is hell. At noon I dial Massé's number, give my name, and ask to talk with him.

"His line is busy. Shall I have him call you?"

"Sure." Trying to be as nonchalant as a man calling about next week's flight schedules, I leave my number.

To keep myself occupied I go outside and take down the storm window at the front of the dining room. I start doing something I've never tried before: to remove the old, disintegrating putty and replace it with new. This is a big window, twenty-five panes in all, and at first I'm so clumsy with the putty and the knife that the job appears to be beyond me. I concentrate hard on following the instructions of the man at the hardware store ("roll each piece of putty in your palms before trying to work it"), and slowly I start to get the hang of it. It becomes what I wanted it to be: mindlessly absorbing. I don't stop waiting for the phone to ring, but being occupied makes the wait barely, barely tolerable.

In the middle of the afternoon Pam comes outside and offers half a dozen plausible reasons why my call isn't being answered. Massé may be waiting for instructions from Imcera Group, she says. Or he may have had to leave his office before he could return my call. I'm grateful for her concern and her efforts to be helpful, mortified to think that my behavior must have made such efforts seem necessary. I reply, aware that at least a trace of anger is showing through, that there is no reason on earth why Massé couldn't have had his secretary call back and promise a real call later.

By late afternoon I'm a puttymaster, moving almost smoothly from pane to pane. Sarah, nineteen years old and on a visit home from college, comes outside and offers her half-dozen explanations of why Massé's failure to return my call isn't necessarily bad news.

"And besides, Dad, this is not the last job on earth. You've got lots and lots of time to find a job."

I thank her and agree that if the job had already been accepted by some other candidate, Massé probably would have had the decency to tell me so. The fact that he's not even taking or returning my calls, however, makes it improbable that I am at this point Imcera's leading candidate. If I've learned anything about headhunters, it's that leading prospects get very good treatment—i.e., aren't left hanging. I've learned too that if you're not in the lead you're close to being nobody.

A light goes on in my head: that's what's going on here. Somebody else is being pursued. Somebody else has been given an offer, and now they're waiting for an answer. I'm a backup, possibly one of two or several backups, held in reserve just in case. Until they get an answer from the one they've chosen, I'm not likely to be hearing anything from anybody.

"Are you going to call them again tomorrow?" Sarah asks.

"I'm not going to call them again ever."

"Good!" she says firmly. She goes back into the house.

I worry about Sarah. Possibly more than any of us, I think, she's been hurt by the turmoil of the past few years. We brought her to Racine just days after her graduation from high school, and she has no connections here. Her summers have been hellishly lonely, which makes me feel terrible. I fret all the more when I see how worried *she* is about *me*.

Wives and children should not be put through this sort of thing. Nobody should be put through this sort of thing. My own nerves feel as though they're at the snapping point. I think of my old parents in St. Louis, my Depression-scarred parents, and how afraid I am that they're going to hear somehow that I've lost my job. I keep hoping I can land a job before I have to tell them that I'm unemployable.

Late in the afternoon the phone rings twice. Still outside, I wait for someone to come to the door and tell me with a meaningful lift of the eyebrows that it's for me. But nobody comes to the door. Not either time.

At the end of the day I wash the putty from my fingers with mineral water and think of Bobby Joyce.

II

HERE'S HOW MUCH I loved the executive life that I've lost and am trying so hard to recover.

I loved it so much that when it was all I had to make a life out of, when home and family and friends and everything familiar had slipped out of reach, my daily life felt nearly like life in prison.

That was in the winter of 1988–89. Early in December I'd left McDonnell Douglas—voluntarily, but under the darkest of clouds, their botched effort to fire me having been followed by a more successful effort to make every day at work an agony—and moved to my new job with J. I. Case in Wisconsin. Pam and I had decided that she should stay behind in St. Louis until June. That way she could extract herself smoothly from her job, helping to find and train a successor. She could try to sell the house. Far more importantly, Sarah would be able to finish her last six months of high school before moving.

And so in the dark depths of winter I found myself living in a furnished apartment in a bleak northern town where I knew no one and had nothing to do but work. Where there was nothing to occupy my time and attention but the slow process of settling into a job, a company, and an industry that were entirely new to me.

And in what a setting! Racine, I eventually learned, can be a kind of paradise in summer. Winter is another story. Every day I went to work before full sunlight and drove back to my apartment in the dark. Daytime was often fiercely cold and even more often sunless and gray. Great slushy dunes of chunk ice piled up along the shore of Lake Michigan.

As for my new job, I found I loved it so much, it gave me so much reason to leap up every morning and go forth, that I started keeping an old paperback copy of Solzhenitsyn's *One Day in the Life of Ivan Denisovich* on the table next to my bed.

On the book's cover was a drawing: a shadowy figure in prison garb, coils of barbed wire, a shape suggesting a machine gun. Turning on the light and pulling myself out of bed, I'd look at it and remember that things could be worse.

Forcing myself into the shower on those black mornings, I'd think about how Solzhenitsyn had survived eight years in the camps. Compared with that, my life was a festival.

Solzhenitsyn made it through eight years of almost never having enough to eat or being able to get warm. He did it without weekends off, or vacations, or the anesthetic of evening television.

What the hell, I'd tell myself: What you're doing isn't even unpleasant compared with that. You ought to be able to hang on for five years, enough to get vested for a bit of pension. Or for eight years, like Solzhenitsyn. Maybe for ten years, even fifteen.

After fifteen years I'd be financially safe forever.

The paperback on my night table was a bit like the crucifixes people keep on their walls. The message was pretty much the same:

If he could do that, surely I can do this.

12

I TALK ON THE phone with an old friend, Bob, and learn that he
and I are going to be in Chicago on the same day. We arrange to
get together for coffee. When he and I first met, we were both
vice presidents of giant aerospace companies. We went trout
fishing together. We even went to the Caribbean together with
our wives. Now we're both on the street.

He's five years or so older than me. That's good and that's
bad. On the bad side it makes him that much less attractive on
the executive meat market. On the good side it puts him that
much closer to the point where the pensions he's qualified for at
two different corporations can start to flow.

He's in town making a pitch for some consulting business. I
know, more from the grapevine than from Bob himself, that he's
been looking hard for a permanent job and getting nowhere.
Now he tells me that next week he's going to be interviewed for a
spot with an outfit in the East. Aerospace again.

"To tell you the truth, I have mixed feelings about it," he says.
"On the one hand it's a hell of a great job. If I took it for five years
I'd be on easy street. On the other hand I just don't know if I want
to get back into the rat race. I really don't know how I want this to
turn out."

I look at Bob and feel certain that he's lying. Like me, he
started out nowhere in life, and I've had a strong liking for him
ever since I discovered that he and I share a lot of the same inse-
curities. I've no doubt that he's as desperate as I am to get himself
planted somewhere, and that this talk about mixed feelings is a
way of insulating himself against another big disappointment. I

feel certain that I know exactly what he's thinking. I've been there. I live there.

I say nothing about this, though. Bob's lie and my silence make me feel sad. They mean that he and I are never going to be much more than business friends.

13

VÁCLAV HAVEL says, in one of his essays, that modern society is held together by fear—by fear of loss, mostly. He says that what we're usually most afraid of losing is our possessions, the things that give us status and make us feel secure.

When we have our fear under control, he says, we shift to greed. To accumulating more and more things with which to assure ourselves that it isn't necessary to be afraid and that our compromises haven't been for nothing.

Havel says, further, that fear drives us to accept corruption and dishonesty, to lie and grovel, to pretend that we are what we aren't and thereby surrender our humanity.

Ultimately, having given away almost everything that matters, we end up defining ourselves by our possessions. This is a degrading thing for a human being to do, and doing it makes us depressed. Gradually all of society becomes gray and dreary and depressed. We become incapable of imagining goals higher or more meaningful than a fine house, a fine car . . .

We abandon hope without even realizing we've done so.

I have friends who wear gold Rolexes and cashmere sports coats, but when you get to know them, it turns out that they regard their own lives as misbegotten messes of fear and greed and disappointment. It's no wonder that so many of these people—people with summer houses and BMWs and three hundred thousand miles of first-class travel in their frequent flier accounts—turn out to be quietly desperate for retirement. I think they see retirement as their last chance to go back to being the people they were when they were starting out, back to being themselves. Too often, though, by the time they reach retirement they're so hollowed out they no longer remember who it is they were. Their idea of fulfillment has come down to six days of golf a week.

How does this happen? It's not easy to say. I'm not at all sure what, if anything, I myself had in mind back when I was starting out.

A few days after my graduation from grade school, following the instructions of an older friend who had already won a place for himself in the world of work, I lied about my age to an elderly pharmacist named Julius Sager and thereby got, at age thirteen, my first regular job. I'd worked earlier than that, selling soda at the circus and hawking newspapers up and down the streets, but my arrival behind the counter at Sager's Drug Store was my introduction to pay by the hour, deductions for Social Security, and all the other paraphernalia of real, regular employment. Given how much of my work life I've spent pretending, it's interesting that the whole thing started with a lie.

Why did I start work at thirteen? Not out of terrible need; this is not a chapter out of *Oliver Twist.* Mostly I did it for spending money that I wouldn't have had otherwise. And because it was what boys did in my world back then. It was expected that when you became capable of paying for your own movie tickets and haircuts and cigarettes, you did in fact start paying for them. In much the same way, it was generally accepted that when you graduated from high school you became responsible not just for your spending money but for supporting yourself, period. Those who went to college earned their books and tuition by stocking shelves at the A&P.

Sager's, the kind of place that provided work for those not old enough for the A&P, was a dying establishment in a decaying, "changing" neighborhood inhabited for the most part by three kinds of people. One group was the dwindling number of the poorest and oldest, and in one way or another the weakest, of the longtime residents, the ones least able to run for the suburbs. Another was a swirling kaleidoscope of the kinds of folks who are called white trash in the South and (for reasons mysterious to me) "hoosiers" in St. Louis; these were people who moved constantly, often going through three or four furnished apartments in the course of a year, seldom outside the boundaries of a single square mile. The third and newest group was rapidly becoming dominant. It was made up of blacks moving in from the Deep South and from the slums being bulldozed for urban renewal a hundred blocks to the east.

Almost from the beginning, and even though I was barely into my teens, I found working at Sager's killingly dreary. It was made worse by rules that seemed to make little sense. It was, in short, an accurate foretaste of the great world of work that I've come to know so well in all the long years since.

At Sager's there were often vast expanses of time—they seemed to stretch for hours, though in retrospect that seems impossible—when not a single customer would set foot in the place. Mr. Sager would sit alone and silent in his narrow back room beneath great overarching shelves filled with brown and green bottles of every size, listening to the Cardinals on the radio or leafing through *Confidential* magazine or just . . . sitting . . . there . . . eternally. Except for the one hour each day when he trudged upstairs for supper with his hard-faced wife, he sat in that back room Monday through Friday from the opening of the store at nine in the morning until ten p.m. arrived at last and we could start locking up. On Saturdays he was there from the start of the day till six, when the same eighty-year-old substitute pharmacist who took his place during his weekday supper hours would report for duty. Sundays were a veritable holiday for Julius Sager: he didn't open until ten, and he closed at four. He'd been keeping this schedule for something like forty years.

It might almost go without saying that Julius Sager was not a joyful man. We boys who worked in solitary shifts as his clerks and soda jerks were not permitted to read or to sit down, no matter how much time went by between customers. Mr. Sager said it would look bad when customers did come in if the help was "lounging around." That was a strange notion, come to think of it. Our most regular customers were hillbilly and black kids who paid for "Exximo pahs" with sweaty nickels. Next door was a dry-cleaning joint operated by a sour old drunk who came in four, five, or six times a day, called out a glum greeting to "Saig" in the back room, and bought two or three bottles of cold beer each time. Then there was the small, fat, more or less youngish woman with uncombed hair who came in most afternoons wearing a bathrobe and house slippers on feet that she dragged from the door to the soda fountain, where she always ordered a nickle Coke. Before leaving she would thumb listlessly through magazines that she never bought. Men you wouldn't want to sit next to on the bus would buy big bottles of cheap wine. Old men would fill their shirt pockets with the cheapest cigars in the case. Taking the trouble to look alert and eager for such customers seemed ridiculous (my first experience of getting paid to pretend, the end of my innocence), but being required to do so didn't seem entirely unfair. Mr. Sager owned the place, after all. And he'd paid his dues, dog-paddling slowly, day after day and year after year, across oceans of tedium too vast for a child like me to imagine.

I felt sorry for Mr. Sager. I've always remembered a night near closing time when he was up in the front of the store and I was in back washing out a sink. A ball game was on the radio. For some reason I looked out over the swinging doors that separated the front from the back and saw him studying his reflection in the dark of the plate-glass window. He was standing between the comic-book racks and the ice-cream freezer, his jaw clenched, his eyes narrow slits. Slowly, thinking he was alone, he took a big windup and delivered an imaginary pitch. It was an odd feeling to be a boy myself and get a glimpse of the boy who was still alive down inside the old prisoner. I'm sure he threw a strike, and that Ted Williams took a big cut at it and missed.

In its way Sager's was a hard place to earn the fifty cents an hour he paid me at the start and the seventy cents I was making when I quit three years later for a job at a suburban supermarket that paid a buck ten. But it taught me why even a job that requires little effort is called "work," and why they have to pay you to do it.

14

Four months now since J. I. Case sent me to outplacement, and still no word from Imcera.

A woman in one of the West Coast offices of Russell Reynolds, the firm handling the search for a p.r. vice president for the San Diego Gas and Electric Company, writes to say that although my qualifications are of course fabulous (I'm now accustomed to being praised extravagantly by everyone who turns me down), I'm not among the candidates the company has decided to interview.

Right.

In the past couple of weeks I've had similar news from a big Philadelphia company called ARA Services, whose headhunter said that though my qualifications are of course fabulous et cetera her clients have decided that the job there requires more experience in the service industry than I can demonstrate.

That's probably fair enough; I don't even know for sure what "the service industry" is.

Imcera aside, I am left with one respectable possibility: Union Camp Corporation, a big paper company in the Northeast. I was interviewed by Union Camp's headhunter several weeks ago. He said he was conducting preliminary interviews with eighteen candidates across the country, and that I was among the most highly qualified. I thought that sounded good and said so.

"It ought to be good," the headhunter told me. "But in this case it could turn out to be a disadvantage. We really haven't settled on the scope of this job, haven't decided how much responsibility it's gonna have. So it's not yet clear what kinds of qualifications they're actually going to want."

Interpretation: I'm "overqualified."

One afternoon, feeling antsy and having nothing more productive to do, I call the Union Camp headhunter to see where that situation stands. He says my call is an amazing coincidence. He was just on the verge of calling me.

Right.

He was going to let me know that Union Camp has decided to "pursue candidates who have more environmental backgrounds."

Right.

Antsier than ever, I write a letter to Imcera Group's headhunter, Larry Massé. Trying to make myself sound calm and jovial, I say I'm sorry we haven't connected recently and am curious to know what's going on. I read the letter to myself over and over again, trying to decide if it sounds weak or sour or snotty. I can't see anything plainly wrong with my draft, but also can't get comfortable with it, so I throw it away and instead write a short note in longhand. "Wondering about the status of the Imcera Group search," I write. "Continuing to believe that it's a solid opportunity in which I could make a real contribution. Hoping to hear from you." This I fax to him—today's way to show serious intent and get attention in a hurry.

No more than an hour later, Massé calls. He does so, inevitably, when I've left my outplacement duty station and gone down the hall to the can. But he leaves his name and number. I call him back and don't get through, gnash my teeth, leave my name and number. He calls again in less than an hour.

He's friendly. "Got your note," he says. "Want to apologize for making it necessary. Been traveling, and other things have been going on, but I'm really sorry if I left you hanging."

His warm tones give me hope.

"It's just as well that I couldn't get back to you till now," he continues. "Imcera has had an offer out to another candidate, and if we'd talked before today I wouldn't have known what to tell you. But now he's accepted, so we can close the loop."

I hold onto enough presence of mind to look down at the little list of questions I've prepared for use in case of bad news.

Who got the job?

"I can't give you the name, because it hasn't been announced. But it's a guy from New York, a guy with experience in chemicals and pharmaceuticals—Imcera's two major lines of business, as you know. He also has master's degrees in both journalism and finance. They just thought his background was a little better suited to their needs."

Is there anything I might learn from this? Did I lay any eggs?

"Not at all, not a bit. I'd let you know if anything of the kind were true. But there were no problems with you at all. They just felt that this other fellow was better suited to their needs."

He adds some things about how glad he is to have met me, how glad to be aware of my existence in case he gets another p.r. search. About how these things happen and this one just wasn't meant to be but the right job is sure to come along soon.

Right.

Nicely we say our good-byes.

I hang up and realize that with Imcera Group gone I am involved in no live searches. I know of some vacant jobs, and in most cases I know the names of the headhunters who are handling them. I've written to all of them, tried to call most of them. Not one of them has given the slightest indication of having the slightest interest in me.

After all these months of trying, after sending out all these hundreds of pieces of mail and making these scores of phone calls, I now have fewer job prospects than I had when the process began.

I am in big trouble.

PART II

Winter 1991

The Questions of a Fatted Calf

15

M TOLD ME TODAY that he's without any job prospects at all and is putting his house on the market; when his separation package runs out it's going to be too expensive to carry.

This is a man whose résumé is cast in gold. He's been executive vice president at two multibillion-dollar corporations, and he's still under fifty. He has an engineering degree and an MBA, is a graduate of the Advanced Management Program at Harvard Business School, and has no disabilities or flaws that I detected in two years of working closely with him. He's been out of work for more than a year now, and he reports that his prospects seem to be narrowing with every passing month. Currently they're near the vanishing point. In the absence of any job opportunities, in the absence of anything to do at all, he's been looking at the possibility of buying some small company somewhere. Always there are complications. Each new company he looks at, he says, is smaller than the last.

"Where's it gonna end?" he asks laughing. "With me running a McDonald's?"

R, a Princeton graduate who has been out of work even longer than M, writes to say that he has packed his eight rooms of furniture into a U-Haul van and moved his entire household, wife and five kids included, from the suburbs of Phoenix to the suburbs of Los Angeles. "I was able to rent the Mesa house," he says. "Wanted to sell it, but no such luck. But I'm hoping I'll be better off in the southern California job market than in Phoenix."

R reports that despite constant effort he hasn't had a serious job interview in more than half a year. A little over a year ago he turned his back disdainfully on a 40K job with a public utility. Now he thinks of it yearningly.

16

I'M LOOKING at one of the few photographs I really treasure, one taken of the Boy Scout troop at St. Mark's school almost forty years ago. In it are nineteen boys, thirteen white and six black, not one with more than a few parts of a complete scout uniform. At the spring camporees, where the entire St. Louis Council assembled, we'd keep an eye out for the troops that looked sharpest. In some, every member not only had complete uniforms but Smokey the Bear hats, official khaki shorts, official knee-length socks. We'd find out where those troops were camped. In the middle of the night we'd swoop down on them, pulling down their tents.

One of my own kids, when I showed the photo to her, said we looked like a pretty tough bunch. I think she was looking at Jerry Nelson, who was my special enemy in grade school and in the picture is cocking his fists as if wanting to duke it out with the camera. What my daughter said made me laugh. We weren't tough at all, actually. We were just punks. It strikes me as funny how, when suburban kids are confronted with city kids, what they see is "tough." They're far too easily intimidated.

Could the boy I was at St. Mark's have imagined the man I am now? I don't see how. Certainly I couldn't have imagined myself having all the success I've had and still ending up at fifty jobless and miserable and so laden with anxiety and dread that I'm astonished not to be leaving two-inch-deep footprints everywhere I walk.

From my first day at Sager's Drug Store to the day I was fired by J. I. Case was almost exactly thirty-eight years. Throughout all those years I was never unemployed. After Sager's came the supermarket. College employment was an erratic progression from the supermarket to a gas station to the post office to a stint as a copy boy on a daily paper to summer work scraping the blubber from sealskins for a fur company in Alaska. Some of these jobs overlapped. I had a lot of jobs in those days, sometimes more than one at a time. I grabbed practically anything that came along.

What's interesting, in retrospect, is that of all my early jobs the best was the one in Alaska, the one where my job title was "blubberer." Physically this was the hardest work I've ever done, bloody and greasy and foul. Five hours of it would exhaust the best of us. And it required living for months on a barren island where the sun literally never broke through the clouds and there were no stores, no movies, no television, no beer, no girls, not even a record player. In the bunkhouse we had one radio, and it picked up just two stations.

But one thing was wonderful about the Alaska job: it had no bullshit to it, no politics, no pretense of any kind. When skins came in needing to be blubbered we worked like brutes, pushing dull knives through resistant tissue as fast as we could until our hands bled. But when we were finished nobody expected us to hang around pretending to be working or pretending to be eager for more. Our job was to finish all the skins on hand as quickly as we could and to avoid damaging them in the process (which is why our knives were dull—that way they wouldn't cut into the skins). As long as we did our job, the bosses were satisfied. When the last skin of the day was inspected and packed away we were free to go back to the bunkhouse and take a long shower and afterward do whatever we wanted—go for a hike, get up a game of poker, fall into bed and sleep. As long as you were good at blubbering (precise records were kept of how many skins you did every day, and of how many skins you damaged), and as long as you didn't cause trouble, they'd invite you to come back again the next year. Blubbering was a good job for some of the same reasons that playing professional baseball was, even back in the days when most big leaguers didn't make a lot of money. Because as long as you could keep your batting average up and work the double play it didn't much matter how you parted your hair or whether you kissed the asses of the people in the front office. Because when the game was over it was over, and nobody expected you to hang around second base looking eager and busy until the clock struck five. And because there was no way of pretending that a really bad ballplayer was a really good one or vice versa.

Sea duty in the Navy was good in that respect: very little b.s. Shore duty was very, very bad.

I read somewhere once that we don't really climb the ladder of success, that if we rise it's almost always because someone has *pulled* us up. That describes my own experience. When I myself have "risen," someone has always been pulling from above. That isn't necessarily a bad thing. If people get pulled up for the right reasons, it can be a good thing. But too often the "successful" people are not the workers, the producers, but the ones willing to do the kinds of dances—the sometimes vile dances—that attract attention upstairs. This also helps to explain the appeal of sports. As long as a man can pitch a dozen winning games of baseball a year or kick a forty-yard field goal against the wind, that man is free to be himself. How many of us, at work, are free to be ourselves?

In my first ten or so years of adulthood, through graduate school and the Navy and Vietnam and my first adult-world civilian jobs, I got accustomed to wearing a necktie and to *being* something rather than simply *doing* something for pay. But through all that I daydreamed about getting free. Until I was well into my thirties I almost always thought of my jobs as interruptions, as intrusions into the parts of life in which I could come closest to being me.

But gradually, by thousands of steps each as insignificant as the twitch of a second hand, we get broken in. By infinitesimal stages we change from rebellious colts to seasoned, stolid wheelhorses. Somehow, gradually, we come not merely to accept the harness but to need it. To be deeply uneasy, even deeply afraid, without it.

Whether that's a good thing depends on whether the load is worth pulling.

This is as far as I feel capable of going in explaining the strange fact—strange considering how little I've enjoyed or been satisfied by many of the jobs I've had—that I now find it so painful to awaken every morning to the realization that I have no work to go to and no one is expecting me anywhere. I think of this before I open my eyes, and the thought always comes as a sharp stab.

Back when I was a colt, shying at the halter and kicking at the traces, I couldn't have imagined all this freedom hurting as much as it does.

17

I'm in New York again, and I decide to look in at the office of a headhunter who has sent me a couple of friendly and vaguely encouraging letters—"Let me know if you're going to be in town" and that sort of thing.

He's with one of the big recruiting firms in offices near the top of one of the really big buildings. When I get to his floor it is, of course, the ultimate in posh. I introduce myself to the receptionist and ask if Mr. Smith is in.

"Do you have an appointment?"

"No, but Mr. Smith knows who I am. He's suggested that we get together, and I'm only in town for the day."

For some reason—the woman's explanation is so smooth it slips away—there's no possibility of seeing Mr. Smith today. The woman suggests that maybe I'd like to talk with Miss Jones, the research specialist. I say sure. By now I know what a researcher does in an headhunter shop: look at the incoming résumés and decide which of them, if any, don't have to go into the trash immediately. It turns out that Miss Jones isn't free either.

I ride the elevator back down to the street and find a pay phone and dial Mr. Smith. I'm told it isn't possible to talk with him. I ask for Miss Jones and am put through to her. I tell her who I am, how I'll be flying out in the afternoon, that I had just been upstairs hoping to see Mr. Smith for a minute or two but hadn't had any success.

"Oh, no," she says, as if I'd just told her of walking up to the gate of the White House and asking to see the president. "He wouldn't have come *out*. They would *never* come *out!*"

Well. Excuse me.

18

No MORE THAN 10 percent of the guys coming out of McBride High School back when I did went on to college. Most of those who did went to Harris Teachers College, the only public institution of higher learning then in existence in St. Louis. I was told by older guys in the neighborhood that to pass freshman phys ed at Harris it was necessary, among other things, to do a flip off a diving board and land on your feet on a wrestling board. This I couldn't imagine attempting, except as a prelude to life in a wheelchair. Thus I found it difficult to imagine going to—or surviving—college.

But in my senior year, to everyone's astonishment including my own, a seemingly endless sequence of Saturday-morning tests led to the blinding news that I'd been awarded a scholarship—no, two scholarships—and had become the first National Merit Scholar in the history of McBride. Briefly, but ever so wonderfully because for the first time ever, I was a celebrity on my block. Not the kind of celebrity I would have chosen to be, not an all-city halfback, but still, it was a lot better than nothing.

Probably it's true that pride goeth before a fall, and no doubt I've committed more than a few sins of pride on the road to where I am now. I can say honestly, though, that I don't think pride came naturally to me. To the extent that it got the best of me it did so slowly, one piece at a time, like some New England stone fence rising glacially over the years. Perhaps the first small piece was dropped into place the day I started high school and found myself assigned to what all of us recognized as the smart guys' homeroom. But I was far more intimidated than pleased by this, and I managed to avoid performing so much as a single act of academic distinction in the course of my freshman year. We took some sort of aptitude test that year. The teacher who gave me my results said they showed me to be woefully lacking in manual dexterity but likely to do well in clerical pursuits. That was his word: "clerical." There was no mistaking the fact that he was talking about my someday becoming a clerk. Nor was I offended or amused. McBride was a small Catholic school run by the Brothers of Mary for the sons of blue-collar families. All of us, teachers and students alike, lived within narrow horizons.

At the end of my junior year, when the formidable black brother in charge of the school paper announced that I was to be the next editor in chief (that was the grand title, editor in chief), I was so completely surprised that along with being thrilled I felt guilty about somehow having cheated harder-working, more earnest, more deserving classmates out of the job. I expected the cheated ones to get angry, to complain, though no one ever did. But mainly what I felt was thrilled and, yes, proud. I think it was my first experience of being what Terry in *On the Waterfront* laments that he never got his chance to be—*somebody, a contender*.

My scholarship lifted me past Harris Teachers College to the highest reaches of American higher education. Or so I thought. I went to Saint Louis University, a private school run by the Jesuits in a collapsing neighborhood two miles west of downtown. The sensible thing to do at "Saint Louie," most people there seemed to agree, was to major in business administration or engineering. I majored in English, partly because I thought any degree would be enough to guarantee my future and partly just because it was what I liked. It took me until my second year to work up enough courage to try for a job on the paper there. When I did so and it took me only three semesters to become the paper's editor in chief (that fabulous title again), I was nearly as surprised as I'd been in high school. And just as pleased, and just as vaguely guilty, and just as proud.

When my work on the college paper led to an offer that made me, at nineteen, the youngest reporter at either of St. Louis's dailies, the offer came without my having sought it or even imagining that such a thing might be possible. When my byline started appearing in the same paper that I'd once peddled from a push-cart back in the old neighborhood (*"Morning Globe!* Getcher *Morning Globe* paaa-per!"*), I wanted to have it blown up and put on billboards. And it may have been when the chairman of the English department nominated me for a big-league graduate fel-lowship and I actually won the thing (I wasn't half sure I wanted it) that I started to think of myself as the kind of person to whom such things happened.

Winning a graduate fellowship and going off to a Big Ten uni-versity for an M.A. wasn't that big a deal in the sixties, obviously. But it *felt* like a big deal.

Becoming a very junior officer in the United States Navy defi-nitely was not that big a deal. But just as nobody in my family had been to college, the men had always gone off to war as pri-vates and come home sergeants. Becoming an ensign and then a lieutenant junior grade felt like another step toward some won-derful unknown.

When I got back from the South China Sea, I went to the Long Beach, California, library and looked up the names of the presidents of the hundred biggest corporations in America. I had no idea what I wanted to do or be, but I assumed that the big companies probably would want to do *something* with somebody like me. I further assumed that going someplace big probably wouldn't be a bad idea. I sent out a hundred letters, enclosing with each a one-page résumé that our Japanese neighbor had printed in his garage. In short order I had offers from New York, Pennsylvania, Delaware, and California.

Getting a corporate job, obviously, was easy.

And when the job I took turned out to be Sager's Drug Store with neckties, I simply walked down the street to the local news-paper and was hired there the same day. *So* easy.

And when after little more than a year with that paper I applied for a job with a bigger, more famous paper, I was again quickly successful. And when after less than two years with the bigger paper I decided to try for a journalism fellowship at Harvard, a fellowship that was supposed to be one of the biggest honors in the American news business, I won on the first try.

I began to think that the higher you climbed, the easier everything got.

Easy? Hey, there was nothing to it. Hey, I was a master of the universe. I was a boy wonder.

In retrospect, I think maybe I was more like a calf being fattened for the kill.

19

I ONCE READ a story in which a young German soldier, shattered by his experiences on the eastern front in World War II, is visited by the ghost of his father. The soldier asks the father, who had been killed in World War I, for help in understanding all the terrible things he has seen.

"How could I know?" the ghost answers. "I'm only nineteen years old! I'm not as old as you are!"

I too have questions. Mostly they're pitiful little questions, and I have the whole world to search for answers. Therefore it seems strange that there is no human being on the face of the earth to whom I feel I can go with a reasonable hope of getting answers.

Where can someone in my situation look for help?

The answer, I think, is nowhere. Actually, in my situation it's all but forbidden to *ask* for help—to let anyone know that you feel the *need* for help. Suppose you learn, for example, that a job apparently well suited to your experience is vacant at the Magma Corporation. You send in your résumé, and in your cover letter you'd like to say not only that this job interests you and that you think you're probably pretty well qualified for it but that, hey, you're hot to trot—out of work for months now, finding it both scary and boring as hell. Give me a chance, you want to say, and I'll show myself to be the most grateful, loyal, hardworking S.O.B. on the North American continent.

Help! you wanna say. Help me and I'll make you glad you did!

But you can't. You just can't. Everybody who's supposed to know says you'd better not.

This question of help gives rise to some of the trickiest little paradoxes in the life of a jobless white-collar worker in the 1990s.

For most of us—the ones who don't have an uncle in the CEO's office at General Motors or an old college roommate who's now under secretary of state—those relatively few people capable of being helpful can be very, very hard to ask. To ask for help is to risk looking lost, pathetic, outside the charmed circle. It's to risk a very hard rejection. It's to risk making yourself look contemptible and therefore unworthy of the very assistance you want and need so badly.

You can try, of course. I tried. When I got into trouble at McDonnell Douglas I bought lunch for a man I'd once worked for, a famously influential p.r. executive whom I'd left voluntarily and with whom I'd stayed on distantly friendly terms over the years. I invited him to lunch because I knew for a fact that he had good jobs to dispense. I told him—being about as candid as it's possible for me to be about such things—that I was in serious need of work.

He said he'd get back to me, and he never did.

This may have been his long-delayed retribution for my departure years before. Maybe down deep he just didn't like or respect me. Whatever the truth about that, the experience was humiliating. It left me with no stomach for exposing my need for the inspection of the powerful in the hope that they will do what they can.

Is that foolish? If you say so. But I'll never try any such thing again. As the Ricky Nelson song says, I druther drive a truck.

On the other hand those relatively few people who really would do anything within their power to help—spouses, parents, children, genuine friends as opposed to business friends—invariably are incapable of offering more than encouragement. You find yourself hating to let them know how needful you feel because most of them are already so worried about you that you're starting to worry about them.

The outplacement folks, of course, are paid to help. The trouble is that you know what they're going to answer before you ask your questions. It's like trying to have a heart-to-heart talk with a book of sermons by Norman Vincent Peale or a videotape from the Dale Carnegie Institute. There's no connection there, no human dimension. No wisdom, for that matter. You're better off talking to yourself.

How long is it possible to remain in a situation like this without starting to crack?

I don't know. How am I *supposed* to know? What I do know is that it's damned difficult to wake up without a job morning after morning for months without starting to feel at least a little uncertain about how capable you still are of going out and playing the executive game with the old aplomb. I suspect that the kind of self-assurance needed in the world of neckties can be as delicate as the frame of a jet plane: treated properly it will last forever, but if something subjects it to unusual kinds of stress the results can be fatal. How long can an ordinary human being survive a steady diet of being rejected out of hand by most prospective employers and rejected after due diligence by all the others? Conceivably forever. Conceivably for another week and a half. I don't know.

What actually happens if you "crack"?

Interesting question. Maybe you burst into tears in the middle of an interview with a CEO. Maybe you start trembling so convulsively you can't shake hands with some headhunter. Maybe you stop bathing, or start screaming at strangers. Maybe your left eyelid starts twitching and never stops. I don't know anybody who has actually broken down under the strain of this in any dramatic way. I've seen some of my fellow outplacement inmates grow more and more silent and strange and show up less and less often to make their calls. I've seen some of them gradually fade away. But a bona fide *breakdown?* Not yet. People are tough.

Is there a way to come out of this mess with a good job but without having had to lie to get it?

Without having had to lie about who I am and what I want and what really interests me, I mean. My definition of a "good" job has become, by now, nastily confused. On one level I mean a job with an impressive title, a fine office, plenty of minions, plenty of good travel, and plenty of pay—things that I've had and lost and would like to have again. On another level I mean, or want to mean, a job that seems worth doing. A job in which, once I get it, I can be myself a good part of the time. Is it possible to go to interviews and spout the requisite rubbish about how what I want most is to be "challenged" and to have the opportunity to make a "contribution" and be a "team player" . . . is it possible to get a job in this way and not have the job itself turn out in the end to be ridiculous?

There's a world of trouble packed into this one little question. It's a question, I'm afraid, that probably answers itself. It's probably the kind of question that, when answered honestly and the answer becomes a basis for action, can get you into a lot of trouble.

I'm not up to dealing with that just now.

Later. Later.

So . . . Am I washed up?

Sometimes I try to ask people this, but always in an indirect way. Not in job interviews, certainly, and not with people I can't afford to expose my weaknesses to—people I might later need to use as references, for example. But sometimes when I'm with somebody who has reasonably good judgment, somebody who knows me and knows something of the world and is a person to be trusted, sometimes when I'm talking with such a person I'll sort of half-jokingly say that I'm beginning to worry that maybe I'm *not* going to find another corporate job, that maybe that part of life is over for me. To this I invariably get a pooh-poohing kind of answer, a quick mention of how fabulous my credentials are and how it's natural to feel discouraged from time to time but utterly unnecessary in a case like mine.

I never find these assurances helpful. What I see—what I've been seeing for years—is the circle formed by the people in this country who have money and security and status getting steadily smaller. At the center of that circle are the people with inherited money, inherited connections, inherited "advantages." Out near the perimeter are people like me, or people like who I used to be, people with good jobs and not much else. What's different today from a few months ago or twenty years ago is that instead of being just inside the circle I'm now just outside it—out here on the same side of the barricades with the people in "service jobs" and the people with no jobs at all and even the people with no address. Many of us are finding ourselves on the outside for the first time. A recession, they call it. But I can't stop wondering if it isn't more than that, if it isn't in fact part of something bigger and worse, an unusually steep part of a long slope down which the American economy has been sliding for a good many years now.

Is it normal to be as afraid as I am?

Am I an ordinarily capable human being coping as well as can be expected with a difficult and painful situation? Or am I a whining weenie?

I care a lot about the answers to questions like these. Who wouldn't? But I don't know where to look for them.

I don't even know who's *entitled* to answer such questions. A psychiatrist? Not any of the psychiatrists I know. A priest? I would have thought so once, but at this stage in life I don't know any priests who seem to know more than I do. My grandma? Possibly. But my grandma has been dead a long time.

Even if this kind of fear is normal, should I keep it to myself?

What about family? Friends? What's fair to them? Is it brave to keep everything inside like some John Wayne, or is it better to let everything out like a good specimen of the New Age? What's healthy? What's authentic?

What's right?

Who can say?

In the history of the world has there ever been a society with so few answers?

20

NETWORKING IS everything, they say. Call everybody you know and build your network. Recruit people to be your scouts, to let you know as soon as they hear of an opening. Get your scouts to give you the names of other possible scouts. Keep reaching, connecting, building.

Two of the prized pieces of my network were Joyce Hergenhan and David Moyer. Hergenhan is the top p.r. exec at General Electric, and therefore a mighty figure in the field. She and I got to know each other when I was in a job much like hers and we were pretty much equals. Moyer is a headhunter who specializes in p.r. jobs. I've known him a long time. I've talked with both of them since losing my job at Case, written to them, counted them among the people I can get tips and leads from.

Today I happened to hear that a very senior p.r. position is vacant at GE. And that Hergenhan has hired Moyer to round up candidates.

Neither has said a word about this to me.

So much for my network.

21

SLOWLY, SLOWLY, my hunt is changing. My expectations are changing.

In the beginning I assumed that I would be moving, later if not sooner, into a job much like the jobs I'd had for the past ten or twenty years. I expected to find—and didn't look seriously for anything except—corporate p.r. jobs that would bring with them a vice president's title and some measure of organizational grandeur. That was the idea behind sending out so many copies of my résumé. That was what I expected when I wrote all those letters and made all my networking calls.

At times I've said, in talking with friends, that maybe I'm never going to find another corporate job. I always say next, in what I hope is a cavalier tone, that if that's how things work out it won't really matter much, not even to me. But until recently this was just bluster. I didn't mean it, didn't really believe that anything of the kind could happen. Now I believe. Now it looks not only possible but likely. And I do think it matters.

Several of the friends I value most have told me from the start of my latest troubles that they hope I never go back into a corporation. *Write*, they advise, *teach*. "My hope is that you'll accept a professorship somewhere and start working on your own writing," the good-hearted woman who used to be my secretary says in a letter. Perhaps she imagines that the world is laying tenured faculty positions at my feet, begging me to say yes. To her, and to other people with a grossly exaggerated view of my market value, I invariably reply that I'll probably end up doing something like what they suggest. But before making a final decision, I add, I owe it to myself to look carefully at all the options. I need to look even into the corporate possibilities, I say, because that's the responsible thing to do.

After some experimentation I settle on the word *responsible* as particularly good in this context. It seems to suggest that though I am of course rich in options, and though of course I know the right thing for me would be a spot in academia or in the world of authors (someplace where I would be free not only to share my wisdom with the human race but to do so in sneakers and sweatshirt), I also need to remember my obligations to wife and children and all that.

Declining to suggest these things would involve an admission that I have at present no options at all, and that as a matter of hard fact I'd grab the first really solid job opportunity that came along regardless of whether it was back in the defense business or back in the agency business or at East Jesus Community College. I don't seem to be capable of that kind of truthfulness. I can't admit how naked I feel and how helpless, can't admit that if anyone gave me one more shot at the fat-cat world I'd snatch at it like a hungry beggar snatching at a dollar bill.

I lie because lying prepares the way for future lies: if I somehow land a new fat-cat job, I can tell friends that of course I was interested in academia, of course I was interested in writing, but this opportunity that's come along is simply too good (not too lucrative, mind you, but too challenging and important and fun) to be passed up.

Lies lies lies.

I make a file for every job lead that comes my way. Each file includes a thin stack of pages: formal job descriptions when I can get them, ads clipped from newspapers, copies of letters sent to headhunters, copies of whatever answers come back from the headhunters who have bothered to reply, brief handwritten records of any phone conversations. At the top of the first sheet in each file I write the name of the company with a red marker. In the early weeks of my search, as the files accumulated, I lined them up in a vertical row on a coffee table in the bedroom, overlapping them, so that the names formed a column.

Early on it was a pretty impressive display. Philip Morris. ARA Services. Digital Equipment Corp. Holiday Inns. Rhone-Poulenc.

Ameritech. Gerber. Imcera Group. Union Camp. Union Carbide. Big, rich corporations. Fat-cat city. At the peak, late last summer, I had ten or a dozen big names lined up on my tabletop, every one of them presumably representing a vacant vice presidency for which I was, presumably, a plausible candidate. It seemed hard to believe, early on, that at least one of them wouldn't lead to an offer of some kind.

Since then my little display of bright red names has withered as completely as the leaves of summer. Gradually, as I've been told or have figured out for myself that I'm not in contention for this job and for that one, I've been moving my files to a cardboard box in the basement. I call the box my department of dead letters.

During the migration of my files to the basement, I found it convenient to broaden my idea of what kinds of leads it would be "responsible" to pursue. Since then I've been answering ads that describe jobs for which I am—or so I honestly believe—ridiculously overqualified. My active leads file now is, in consequence, as fat as it's ever been. But it's fat with jobs I would have sneered at in June, July, or August.

I now have a file on something called the National Fertilizer Solutions Association, which ran a small ad for a communications manager in the *St. Louis Post-Dispatch*. I found the ad while checking the Sunday newspapers at the Milwaukee public library, answered it, followed up with a fax. A man there called and said he wants to talk. I'm going to take him up on that. It's an excuse to run down to St. Louis and see my parents and my son. And it's better than having no place to interview at all.

I also now have a file on a magazine-editing job with the American Bar Association (it ran for weeks in the *Chicago Tribune* and undoubtedly drew a thousand responses) . . .

On an unnamed corporation that ran an ad for a public relations director ("Blind," I've labeled this one, since I haven't even been able to find out what company it is), and . . .

And on three public relations agencies trying to fill jobs conspicuously less exalted than the agency job I left sixteen years ago . . .

I have a file on a job with a company that appears to be in the natural gas business in some way that its ad doesn't quite make clear in a place called Dublin, Ohio . . .

On a job with something called HCI Publications in Kansas City . . .

On a Washington-based association called the NRECA (I answered the ad without taking the trouble to find out what the acronym means—solid proof of the intensity of my interest) . . .

On Boston College, which ran an ad for a director of public relations . . .

And on the Columbia University Press, which is looking for a sales representative to cover, by automobile, at an annual salary of less than thirty thousand dollars, a region extending from Illinois to Texas.

One of my motives in answering such ads is to get a better sense of what kind of response will get me an offer of an interview and what won't. The answer, so far, seems to be that almost nothing I do leads to an interview.

Most of these ads ask for two things: a résumé and a salary history. I know that most of the people who read the answers would laugh if I told them how much I've been earning these past ten or fifteen years. So in some cases I simply ignore the question. In others I write that salary history is irrelevant "because what I'm looking for is a challenging opportunity with a dynamic organization that sets high standards and is looking for excellent performance," et cetera et cetera, blah blah blah. What am I supposed to do? Give them information that is sure to put me out of contention? Decline to pursue the only leads I can find?

When I complain about not getting answers when I answer ads of this kind, Pam says I'm being ridiculous. People are simply not going to look seriously at someone so obviously overqualified, she says.

She's right, I'm sure. But again, what am I supposed to do? Sit here waiting for someone to call about a job that is "worthy" of me? I see now that I could wait forever. Literally. I could become a modern equivalent of Miss Havisham in *Great Expectations,* sitting here year after year watching a canopy of cobwebs form over my telephone.

Slim pickings.

22

SOMEBODY SUGGESTS that I meet a woman named Linda Stephenson, the dominant partner in a Milwaukee p.r. agency called Zigman Joseph Stephenson. I write and enclose a résumé. I tell her I'm looking for something new.

Her secretary calls back and schedules a lunch. Stephenson brings along the firm's oldest active partner, a sweet-faced and somewhat abstracted man named Jules Joseph. (Zigman, whoever he was, is no longer on the scene.)

Linda Stephenson has a good reputation, and I find that I like her. The two of us spend an hour talking about the p.r. game. Jules Joseph, who must be close to eighty, sits between us and says hardly a word. He seems to enjoy his food.

Stephenson tells me that Joseph is interested in retiring, and that both of them are interested in finding someone to buy him out. I say I'd be interested in exploring the possibility. She says there's another partner, a man named Peterson. She'd like me to meet Peterson and will call soon to arrange another meeting.

The second meeting is scheduled quickly. But when the day arrives and I'm putting on my necktie, the phone rings. There's been an emergency of some kind, and Stephenson and Peterson have to go see a client. Somebody will call me shortly to reschedule.

This is followed by two months of silence. At last I call Stephenson's office. Somebody I don't know calls back and schedules a breakfast meeting, and this one comes off. Again Stephenson and I talk easily. This time we go into more detail about the idea of my buying a partnership. Peterson, a thin and intense young man, is the silent partner this time. He seems neither interested nor amused. He does not appear to be enjoying his food.

I ask Peterson if he has any concerns. Yes, he says. He's concerned that I might use their phones and their office space while rounding up a stable of clients, then take my clients and walk away. I tell him I have nothing of the kind in mind. Not joking, I tell him that I only wish it were that easy to round up clients. It's a good thing I'm not joking, because he is not amused.

Stephenson has apologized repeatedly for failing to get back to me for such a long time. She has offered explanations. I tell her that no harm has been done, but that I do need to make some decisions about my future soon. I say I'm still interested and would be grateful if she could let me know—soon, this time—whether the partners want to pursue the matter further.

She assures me that she too is interested, and that this time it won't take long. I can depend upon hearing from her within the week, she says.

I never hear from her again.

Bad breath, do you suppose?

Do I perhaps chew with my mouth open?

23

AFTER DARK, carrying some clothes out to the car for the trip to St. Louis, I fall into conversation with my neighbor, the one I'm always envying when I hear him drive off to work in the morning. Jim is an industrial engineer with an MBA, the manager of a small manufacturing operation owned by Europeans. He crosses the Atlantic frequently, sometimes taking his wife. I used to do such things; now I stay at home and masticate my jealousy like a steer with its cud.

Seeing me loading things into the trunk of my car, Jim asks if I'm on my way out of town. "In the morning," I say. "I've got an interview lined up."

"Ah!" Jim snorts. "What you wanna do *that* for?"

I sort of shrug, not knowing what he means and not knowing what to say. He knows I've lost my job. Why should he be scornful because I've managed to get an interview? "I've just this evening told my boss," he says, "that I want him to try to find something for me to do that won't take more than two or three days a week. I've had it."

"Really? You really *did* that?"

Yes, Jim says with a nod, he really did. Behind him and just above his head a light is on. I can barely make out his face, but it's clear that he's not joking and that he's pleased with himself.

"Well, you know, it's funny, I know exactly what you mean," I say. "One of the main things I've come to realize is that if I were ten years older I wouldn't even *try* to find another corporate job. I go to these goddamn interviews and try to do my best, but all the time a little voice in the back of my skull is telling me, 'You know you don't really want this job. You know you don't want to do this anymore.' But I'm just not in a position, financially, to do anything about it."

"You can scale back. I figure that if I try working two or three days a week and it doesn't work out, I can switch to teaching—something like that."

We talk awhile longer, mainly about something in today's news. The new management of J. I. Case, the company that brought me here to Racine, today announced a third-quarter loss of more than six hundred million dollars. It's nearly unbelievable, considering the size of the company, that it could be hemorrhaging two hundred million dollars a month.

"You know they didn't really lose *that* much," Jim says. "But the new guys are still so new that nobody's going to blame them for anything yet. That means they can make things look as bad as they want right now and take no heat at all. They'll take hunks of that six hundred million and squirrel some of it away here, some of it there. Next year they'll start drawing on it to make their profits look better than they are. They'll be big heroes, big turnaround artists. What bullshit."

I laugh and ask how his business is doing.

"Oh, it's fine, fine. But they don't want to do anything except the routine stuff—whatever's most profitable right now. I tell them we need to invest in some things and they say, No, we don't want to invest in anything. I'm sick of it."

We start heading for our doors.

"See you later," I say.

"It's all bullshit," says Jim without looking back. "All bullshit."

24

THE FIRST THING I do when I get to St. Louis is take a big sweeping detour out to Kirkwood, the suburban town where Pam and I lived for twenty years. Driving past what used to be our house, I struggle with the thought that I'm a mere visitor here, a passer-by. Somebody whose name I don't know has painted my front door and shutters a new color. It looks good, and I hate it. The pain I'm feeling is so great that it seems my torso ought to be wrapped in bandages. It seems unnatural that with all this pain, blood isn't pooling on the seat of my car.

Later, when I get to my parents' house and ring the bell, my mother comes to the door as usual. My father, as usual, stays in his chair in front of the television. He's just finished a course of radiation therapy. Now in their eighties, the two of them are so frail they seem to have been constructed from rolls of parchment.

I've decided that I have to tell them about the loss of my job. Otherwise, I'm afraid, they'll hear about it through the family grapevine. However they hear it, I'm sure, the news is going to frighten them. These are two people whose early lives were badly twisted by the Depression. Both of them—but especially my mother, who never graduated from high school—have been waiting all their lives for the Depression's return. Their little house was paid off decades ago, they're collecting Social Security and a post office pension plus a monthly pittance from the Teamsters, and by any measure they appear to have come through safely after all. But I feel certain that news of what's happened to me is going to be a blow to an inner place where old wounds have never healed. Better that they hear it from me, with whatever reassurances I can offer, than in the course of idle conversation with a cousin.

Since June I've been carefully misleading them, calling them every week or two as usual and pretending that I'm calling from my office. Occasionally my father, who reads every page of his daily paper with scholarly care and knows much more about the economy than I wish he did, asks how business is. Lately he's been asking every time I call, and recently he sent me a newspaper clipping about the growing financial problems of J. I. Case, the company he thinks I'm still working for. The article made reference to huge losses and to staff cuts. "This is distressing," he wrote in a tremulous hand so different from the astonishingly beautiful handwriting he'd had until becoming so old.

Clearly he knows that all is not well. Probably he suspects that things are worse than he knows. He graduated from high school in 1929—was such a good student that he finished a year early—tried to go to college, couldn't find the money. The thirties turned out to be hard times for him. For a while he chopped down trees for a dollar a day. He's entitled to be afraid.

"Terrible!" I always say in a bluff and cheery tone when he asks about business. "Stinks!" A more positive answer wouldn't be credible and wouldn't prepare him for the truth. "Ah, but what can you expect these days?" I add, trying hard to sound devil-may-care. "We'll be okay."

From the beginning I've been hoping it won't be necessary to tell him or my mother anything until after I've landed a new job. In my imagination I send them a copy of an offer letter, the terms of a vice presidency offered by Imcera Group or Gerber Products or somebody else. To the copy of my offer letter I attach a handwritten note. "Obviously I couldn't turn this down—especially with things so bad in the equipment industry!" And with that everything is settled.

Daydreams.

Half an hour after supper I join my parents in the minuscule room that once was my bedroom and later was my sister's and now is barely big enough for the three chairs, the sewing machine, and the big Sony television they've arranged against the walls. They're watching a sitcom. I sit down and start leafing through the news-paper.

"Do you ever watch this show?" my mother asks.

"Uh, sometimes, I think, yeah." I have no idea what show it is.

"It's pretty funny. We watch it all the time."

"Huh," I say, staring at the screen and nodding in such a way that my answer will fall, ambiguously, somewhere between Whatever You Say, Mom and I agree.

This house is so small, so dominated by the habits of these two people, that it's like a shell they've grown together. I have trouble remembering how four of us lived in it at the same time. I sit here watching for my chance to deliver a piece of news unlike any I've ever brought here before. On the walls around us are photos. My parents in my father's front yard on the day of their wedding, the two of them dressed not in white gown and morning coat but as though they were setting off for work in some upscale office. My sister and me, I in my senior year of college with a tight-knotted narrow tie and oiled-down short hair, she in the white cap and high, sprayed-stiff hair of a new nursing-school graduate in the late sixties. My grandmothers and grandfathers, my parents' grandsons and granddaughters. Embroidered slogans in picture frames.

The sitcom ends and my father jabs at his remote control, killing the sound of the commercials.

"I see in the paper," I say, "that they're laying off fifteen hundred people at Southwestern Bell."

"Yeah," says my father, "and over in Red Bud they're closing some plant where six hundred and fifty people work. Seems like there's something like that happening every day."

"Thank God the recession is over," I say, making sure to laugh as I say it.

"How are things at your place?" my father asks.

"Not so good, really. Actually, business is damned bad." We're all silent for a moment, my parents keeping one eye on a silent commercial for some automobile. "That's something I've been wanting to talk to you about."

They turn toward me big-eyed, frozen, like a couple of deer that have suddenly smelled mountain lion. What do they expect to hear?

That Pam and I are getting divorced? That I have some fatal disease?

Bringing bad news to ancient parents is, I'm finding, a great deal like talking with headhunters. The essential thing in both cases is to be calm, confident, absolutely self-assured. Or to *seem* so: to keep less orderly feelings totally out of sight.

"Listen, I've lost my job." Their eyes seem to get bigger. I pause, feeling as if I've just confessed to an ax murder. When nobody falls down dead I go on. I talk for a long time. I go through the problems that brought the J. I. Case Company to the verge of ruin—the decision to keep the assembly lines humming even after sales began to drop, the huge losses rising out of this decision, the unexplained departure of the president, the sudden dismissal of two executive vice presidents, the progressive elimination of more and more jobs and then of whole departments. The addition of my job, finally, to the list of those being eliminated.

"I knew something was wrong," says my father. "I sent you that article."

I tell them I'm still drawing my salary, will continue to do so for a good while longer, won't be financially desperate even if I'm still out of work when the checks stop coming. I tell them a little about separation packages, golden parachutes, outplacement, the things that corporations commonly do nowadays when relatively senior people are made to walk the plank.

"Why do they *do* that?" my mother asks. Golden parachutes are a strange concept for a woman who learned to operate an office machine called a comptometer as a girl and made a living out of it in offices across St. Louis for more than half a century. Her final years of full-time work were in a dairy office where she had to join the Teamsters. That qualified her for her only pension, sixty-six dollars a month.

"I'm not sure why, really. It's just the way the world works these days. Partly, I guess, because they realize that these things aren't the fault of the people losing their jobs. Partly because the people who haven't lost their jobs yet know it could happen to them. Partly it's just the old story: them that has, gets. And partly, I guess, it's a sort of substitute for job security."

"There's no such thing as job security anymore," says my father.

"No, and there's no such thing as loyalty either."

"Naw."

I tell them things I've never told them before about money. Not a lot, but much more than my usual silence on the subject. What I do, mainly, is color in the bright parts of the picture and ignore the dark parts. I say nothing about the sums—sums that even I still find almost unimaginable at times—that have been flowing out of our checking account every month year after year to keep the kids in school, the house and the cars going, all of it insured, the IRS satisfied . . . I myself don't want to think about how quickly this monthly nut will sink us when my separation package runs out.

These are sums that I've been dealing with for years, and they still knock me back when I look at them closely. If I told my parents what they add up to in a year's time they'd either decide I couldn't possibly be serious or lie down to catch their breath. I saw my father's federal income tax return the year I graduated from high school. His gross income was under five thousand dollars. The taxes on my house are now over seven thousand dollars a year and rising scarily. I skip over all that.

They appear to be satisfied with what I've said. Their attention drifts back to the television. Everything is fine—except that I seem to be just as alone as I was at the beginning of the conversation. My parents know, now, that the wonder boy is unemployed but coping. They've no idea how the wonder boy is feeling, and it's not clear to me that they care.

My father turns in. My mother asks what I'm doing with my time now that I'm not going to an office every day. I try to explain how much time it takes to look for executive work the modern way. I say half jokingly that I'm playing a little more golf than usual too, and enjoying the chance to take things a little easy.

Enjoying?

"You know," I say, "there's only one thing about this whole situation that really worries me at all."

"What's that?" my mother asks. Instantly she's tightened up again.

"The only thing that worries me, really, is that *you're* going to be worried. Other than that, everything is fine. If you just won't worry about me, I won't have a thing to worry about in the world."

This finishes the job of putting her at ease. I have a beer and she has a glass of wine and after a while I go to bed. I lie in the dark in a house where I first lived as a fifteen-year-old and wonder if my parents have any idea at all of what is going on inside me.

What a ridiculous question. I just went to great lengths to keep them from knowing what's going on inside me.

I wonder if the only thing they care about, all they need for peace of mind, is the certain knowledge that the wonder boy isn't going to turn out to be a burden or an embarrassment.

What a question. Where do these questions *come* from?

I make a trip to the bathroom. Through an open door I see that my mother has fallen asleep with her lamp burning and her eyeglasses on and a copy of the *Reader's Digest* open at her chin. She has some pink plastic thing covering her hair, and her teeth are out. For once she shows her eighty years. I put her magazine and her glasses on the table and turn out the lamp.

When I'm back in bed new questions rise to the surface of my mind.

Could the intensity of my unhappiness be explained, in part at least, by the sheer foolishness of the life I've been living?

Could this submerged resentment of mine, this sullen wondering about whether my parents even care about my troubles, could all of it be explained at least in part by the fact that for years now I've been living a life far different from the life I would have, should have, chosen?

Instead of living a real life, have I dreamed one up for myself—one in which I do the things I think other people want me to do?

Could that be why I'm so miserable now? Because it's time to wake up, and I don't want to?

Is that why I hate the headhunters so much? Not because they're as bad as I want to believe they are, not even because I have to grovel at their feet, but because I'm groveling at their feet for something I don't regard as being worth it?

If I'm on the wrong road, if I've been on the wrong road for half or a third of my life, am I still capable of finding the right one?

What *is* the right road?

What a mess.

25

WHAT WAS supposed to be an interview with the guy at Fertilizer Solutions Association turns into a two-day visit. The head man, a bright and bluff ex-farmer named Jim Boillot, starts by entertainingly telling me the story of how he went bust in the agricultural crash of the early eighties, got a political appointment in the U.S. Agriculture Department for a while, and finally took the job he has now as a way of getting back to Missouri. It's clear, though, that he enjoys his work and cares about it. He seems to enjoy talking with me. He also seems to be taking me seriously.

The job I'm a candidate for, unfortunately, is mostly a matter of writing and managing a magazine that's entirely devoted to the subject of liquid fertilizers. That isn't a dishonorable subject, certainly, and my recent experiences with headhunters and outplacement definitely have deepened my experience of things closely akin to fertilizer. But it does sound faintly ridiculous.

Boillot wants his staff to meet me, and so on the first day he arranges for three of his people to take me out to lunch. One, a man whose main job is selling ads in the magazine, talks about how he himself recently went through a long and painful search for work.

"There are so few jobs these days," he says. "And so many people looking. Employers are drawing the most incredibly fine distinctions. If you're a widget salesman and learn about a vacant job at a widget company, what you end up being told is, 'Well, obviously you've got a good record, but all your experience is in *blue* widgets. We really need to find somebody with experience in *blue and white* widgets.' It's incredible out there."

I assure him that I, too, have found it to be incredible.

When I meet with a man whose main responsibility is recruiting new members for the association and making sure they're satisfied, I learn that he, too, is on the staff, having been laid off earlier in the year by a collapsing soybean association. After that I meet the staff lawyer, another recent arrival, a fiftyish man with photos of his large family on the sill behind his desk. He tells me—I'm amazed by how frank all these people are about their recent catastrophes—how he had been an investor in and manager of a string of discount gas stations that went under. I ask, wondering if I have the right to ask, whether he plans to stay with the fertilizer association permanently. Probably not, he says. "Don't get me wrong. It's a good place. Nice people. But it just doesn't pay what I'm going to need in the long term. I took it because at the time I needed a job. Needed a job bad." He smiles when he says this.

I don't tell him I know the feeling. This whole place is a collection of refugees, apparently. We seem to be evolving into a nation of refugees. Native-born refugees.

At the end of the second day (I've been trying to break away, but there's always somebody else I'm told I absolutely have to meet) Boillot takes me back into his office for a final talk. He explains how important the magazine is to his operation. It's a highly profitable venture—so profitable that if subscriptions or ad revenues fell off severely the entire association would be crippled. It's essential that the magazine be interesting, that it deliver something of real value to people who make their living in the world of liquid fertilizers. This is very different from some corporate house organ. This is real.

He's sure I could bring talent and good experience to the magazine, Boillot says. He has a concern, though: I've never run a publication of this kind, one that has to hold paying subscribers and turn a profit. Could I do it? He says he's sure I could. Could I do it well from the day I reported for work? He needs to think about that, he says. He can't afford much of a learning period, and he can't afford much risk.

I tell him I think I can do what he needs done and do it from the first day. But I don't argue hard. Though I like this man, I know already that if he offers me the job I probably won't accept. Probably *shouldn't* accept, because almost certainly I'd feel out of place in it and therefore probably would start resenting the cut in pay I'd be taking almost from the day I arrived.

I don't tell Boillot these things. I shake his hand and thank him for everything, get into my car and head back to Wisconsin. A few mornings later he calls and tells me that he's found a candidate who has spent years running a magazine almost exactly like the fertilizer association's. "I just don't think I can justify not hiring him," he says. I agree effusively (hoping that he'll think me the soul of magnanimity for doing so) and thank him again. He asks me to let him know wherever I go in my next job, and I promise to do so. When I hang up it's with a feeling of relief; not getting an offer means I won't have to agonize over whether to take a job that obviously would be wrong for everyone involved, won't have to turn this good man down after taking up two days of his time.

Funny to be turned down and feel so good about it. Funny how the two days I spent with Boillot and his people feel like time well spent. Funny, after so many foggily ethereal interviews for corporate jobs, how clearly I can remember the things we talked about at the Fertilizer Solutions Association.

Funny to be shown in this unexpected way that it isn't really necessary for the hiring process to be so phony.

26

I GET HOME ON Thursday afternoon and learn that I've had a call from a man named Lewis Hanson.* The message says he works for a firm whose name I recognize—a big headhunter shop in downtown Chicago. I know I've sent them my résumé. It's been a while since I've had a call from a headhunter.

"He was nice," Pam reports. "Friendly. He left his office number and his home number, and he said if you don't reach him before the weekend starts you shouldn't hesitate to call him at home."

Immediately I try Hanson at his office and don't reach him. I try on Friday and again don't reach him. On Saturday at noon I try his home number; a small child says he isn't there but probably will be there in an hour. I wait an hour and a half and try again and am told by a child that Hanson was there a little while ago but has left to have lunch "at the club."

I leave messages, but Hanson doesn't call back. On Sunday at noon I call again. This time a woman tells me that Hanson isn't there but probably will be there in an hour. I ask if I'll disturb anyone by calling back. She says no, calling back will be fine. I give my name, ask her to tell Hanson that I've called and will call again. When I call again I get no answer. At six and again at seven in the evening I get no answer.

On Monday morning, embarrassed about all my calls and messages, I nevertheless try again. I call Hanson at his office, fail to connect, leave my name and number, decide to forget the whole thing.

In the afternoon Hanson calls back. He apologizes for not getting back to me sooner, says something apparently having to do

---

* *A pseudonym.*

with his being divorced or separated. He's not living with his wife or ex-wife and children, evidently, and doesn't always get the messages that are left for him.

I, of course, am Mr. Amiability. Didn't get back to me? No problem! I'd hardly noticed! And what can I do for you this fine day?

What I can do for Lewis Hanson, it turns out, is tell him if I know of any vacant p.r. jobs or any searches in progress. He, it turns out, once worked in jobs in some way connected to corporate communications. Now he wants back in. He's looking for leads himself. I have to laugh.

He does, it turns out, have a tip to share with me: Gerber Products has a search on. After my misadventures with Gerber and its headhunter I really do have to laugh.

Hanson and I agree to keep in touch and continue exchanging tips. Eventually, at his suggestion, we agree to meet for lunch in Chicago. I call at his office, where he leads the way to a garage and a big black Mercedes—about as practical here in the Loop as it would be in midtown Manhattan—and drives us to an expensive seafood restaurant. He talks constantly as he drives, dropping one big name after another. Mr. Connections. If I didn't already know what a wide net he's casting in search of a job I'd probably be impressed.

He has turned out to be a beaten-up-looking guy with a bald, bullet-shaped head. He says something jokey about looking forward with dread to his fiftieth birthday. I immediately go into a funk at the thought that this man who appears to be half as old as God is actually younger than I. How could that be? What do *I* look like to other people?

To be polite, or maybe just to have something to say, I observe that headhunting—"executive recruitment"—seems to be an interesting way to make a living. "The guys who are really established," I say, "seem to be on top of the world."

"Don't kid yourself," Hanson says. "Things are tough in this business too. Nobody wants to say so, but these are hard times for headhunters. There just aren't that many searches." He starts laying out what I become afraid is going to be a long string of details about what I ought to do if what I really want is to get into the headhunting game.

"I didn't really mean it that way," I say, interrupting. "I just meant it looks like an interesting way to make a buck. For myself, I think I'd better stick with what I know."

Hanson gives a little shrug and turns back to his swordfish. I'm a p.r. man, he's a headhunter—obviously my aspirations are of little interest to him. I lower my nose into my beer and wonder what I'm doing here.

Somehow I get stuck with the bill.

27

At one time in my life I was a teacher. During my years as a newspaper reporter I moonlighted as an English teacher, first at a university where most of my students were puppylike young Wasps, later at a community college where my classes were largely made up of skeptical, street-shrewd city blacks.

I enjoyed being a teacher, and I think I was good at it. The administrators who sometimes sat in on my classes and wrote my evaluations never failed to say I was good at it. My students almost always seemed interested, and they generally seemed to learn what I wanted them to learn. In my composition classes I experimented with different ways of teaching students to write, and some of my experiments got terrific results.

Once, at the community college, a big thirtyish black man who had been in my class the previous semester stopped me in the hall. He wanted me to know, he said, that he and another guy who had also been in my class had been asked by their current English teacher where they had learned descriptive writing. From Meyer, they said. It was impressive, the other teacher said. I've always remembered that with pride.

Maybe I could be a teacher again. Maybe I could be a teacher full-time and permanently.

Then again, maybe I couldn't.

I've checked out high school teaching, and it looks like a blind alley. The first problem—aside from what I've heard and read about students with guns, students on drugs, students who can't read and don't care—is that to get a job you have to be certified. You have to get a license from the state. And to do that you have to take courses (usually a big number of courses) in education. Which are widely known to be just about the dumbest courses in the history of the human race.

Getting certified would take a lot of time and therefore a lot of money. Worse, I've learned that the market for English teachers has dried up just about everywhere. Especially for retreads trying to break into the field. I could spend a couple of years getting my ticket punched, use up a big piece of my net worth in the process, and never get a job.

I'm motivated, but I'm not a masochist.

Are there any jobs in college teaching? To find out I wrote recently to the heads of the English departments at every college and university within an hour's drive of home. Some of my letters were never answered. Some were answered in the same way corporations answer such letters if they bother to answer them at all: thanks for writing, you're wonderful, we'll keep your stuff on file in the unlikely event that something suitable turns up, et cetera.

But at the University of Wisconsin's huge Milwaukee campus there's a whole big department-within-the-English-department responsible for teaching freshman composition. The biggest problem facing the director of this composition factory is finding all the teachers he needs without rupturing a painfully limited budget. His answer is a common one in higher education these days: he hires lots of part-timers for low pay and no benefits. One byproduct of this approach is high turnover. The lucky part-timers move on to full-time spots elsewhere, and most of the others eventually wear out and fade away.

In his desperation for fresh manpower the director invited me to come in for an interview. Ten minutes after we shook hands he was asking me how many sections I was willing to take. He was prepared to let me have two, even three if I wanted them. Apparently I could have a full-time load so long as I didn't harbor fantasies about a full-time salary or benefits.

I told him that one would do for starters; even three wouldn't amount to a healthy fraction of a living wage. Better to find out what I was getting into, I thought, before getting in too deep.

What I was getting into, I soon found, was pay that barely justified the drive to campus and demands on my time that were
nearly without limit. I would be required, before the start of the
semester, to attend a full week of orientation. After that, I would
be expected to spend four hours a week in continuing training.
I'd also have to maintain generous office hours. Not to mention
actually teaching my section three times a week and grading the
papers.

I thought about bailing out but decided to give it a try. Then
orientation began, and on the first day I began to see just what it
was that we composition instructors were expected to do. The
director started telling us about something I'd never heard of—his
term for it was "group composition." Each class was to be divided
into clusters of six or eight students. We would then give writing
assignments to these little squads rather than to individuals, and
expect them to collaborate in . . .

Group composition? If some college had tried to teach one of
my own kids group composition, I'd have demanded my money
back.

During the lunch break I took an agitated walk around the
block and tried to figure out what I should do. I found the
director, told him a great ripe lie about how I'd suddenly and
unexpectedly been offered a job down in Illinois, and with ful-
some apologies said that this would make it impossible for me to
teach even part-time in Milwaukee. Then I got out of there.

And that was the end of that. So much for teaching.

28

No COMPANY has ever courted me as ardently as Abbott Laboratories. It happened in the early eighties, and it was flattering. They drove me around in limousines and put me and Pam up at the Deer Path Inn in Lake Forest. Then they offered me a beautiful package. Turning them down was hard, and when I did turn them down they came back at me asking why, asking what they could do to change my mind.

Recently I've been thinking, naturally, that if I'd said yes I'd probably be a lot better off. Abbott has been a remarkably successful company these past ten years.

Today I went to a seminar on how to set yourself up as a professional consultant. My attendance was arranged by the outplacement geeks, and everybody there was recently deceased. When the seminar began we went around the table in the usual way, introducing ourselves.

Guess who the elegant-looking guy seated to my right turned out to be? A recently deceased vice president of public relations. From Abbott Labs.

Small world.

29

I NEARLY WENT to law school once. I took the Law School Admission Test, took a couple of political science courses to get myself ready, found the courses uninteresting but still wrote to law schools for application forms. I didn't really want to do it, though, and in later years when I had the opportunity to witness lawyers at work I wasn't sorry not to be doing what they were doing for a living.

Naive as it may sound—yes, I know the stories about how deeply unhappy so many lawyers supposedly are these days—I now wish I'd gone to law school. I might by now have a secure practice no one could take from me. A guy I knew in college went to law school, went into practice after graduation, eventually decided that he hated it, and by his own cheerful admission spent years kissing the asses of politicians in an effort to get himself made an administrative judge handling Social Security disputes. This year, finally, the smooching paid off. Now he has lifetime possession of an uncomplicated job where nobody can hurt him. Ironclad lifelong security. Sounds good to me.

I didn't go to law school because unexpectedly I was nominated for, and then unexpectedly won, a fellowship for graduate work in English. I went off to spend a year getting an M.A. because it sounded like more fun than going to work or to law school, and because it was a chance to find out whether academia was the place for me (I quickly decided that it wasn't). Then, coming out of grad school, I joined the Navy to avoid the draft. That led to Officer Candidate School, a year and a half on a destroyer patrolling the coast of Vietnam, and a final, screamingly pointless year at a Navy supply depot in southern California.

My first job after the Navy was a vague one—my title was "administrative editor," reflecting the fact that I wasn't quite an administrator and wasn't quite an editor—with Meredith Publishing Company in Des Moines. Meredith was a gigantic outfit as publishers go, producing a zillion copies a month of *Better Homes and Gardens* magazine, nearly that many copies of *Successful Farming*, and profitable lines of cookbooks and do-it-yourself books and other forms of printed retail merchandise. The company was listed on the New York Stock Exchange, it was engaged in presumably creative kinds of work, and as a place to work it proved to be an almost heartbreaking disappointment.

I had a cubicle deep inside the company's massive old brickwork headquarters and very little to do. Most of us had very little to do. My boss, who had the title of editorial director, had a real office with a real door and real floor-to-ceiling walls but not much more to do than I had. I would peek into his office as I crept away for one of my incredibly long coffee breaks and see him, pencil in hand, staring intently down at a blank sheet of ruled notebook paper on his desk. An hour or two later, sneaking back to my office, I would peek in again. I would see him in exactly the same position, still gripping his pencil and still gazing at what was, I'm certain, the same piece of blank paper. All this was especially maddening because I regarded myself, out of school and out of uniform at last, as on the threshold of my career. I wanted to get started. I wanted to do things. Being hired and then left so idle felt like a betrayal.

Everybody at Meredith was bored half insane, and gradually I learned to separate my associates into two groups. One, by far the largest, was made up of earnest sorts determined to stay in the role of the serious executive under all circumstances; they had as little to do as any of us but insistently pretended to be constantly challenged. It was easy to identify these people: I'd make a glancing, joking reference to the tedium of the place, and they were the ones who gave back a blank stare lightly flecked with annoyance. It was like being in a Bela Lugosi movie, suddenly flashing a crucifix at somebody and seeing him flinch. "Ah, yes, obviously this one's a vampire!" Ah, yes, I would tell myself, obviously there's no life left in this one. Obviously there's no point in trying to connect with this one.

Flaubert said that "to be stupid, and selfish, and to have good health are the three requirements for happiness—though if stupidity is lacking, the others are useless." Most of these co-workers of mine, alert and educated American executives, editors, and marketers, kept themselves in a state of dry Flaubertian happiness by willfully rendering themselves stupid. The price was a heavy one. Their motto could have been Death to Irony. Or Death to the Human Spirit. That was corporate life in the bloated and bountiful sixties, long before anyone dreamed of such a thing as "downsizing."

Gradually, here and there, I made the acquaintance of a small number of people (all of them were male—anything else would have been unusual in midwestern junior executivedom at that time) who didn't recoil when I flashed my secret signal but instead flashed theirs back. These were the people who saw the place the way I did and were willing, whenever it was minimally safe, to say so.

Eventually a few of us formed a kind of secret cell that would meet every morning and every afternoon in a remote and cavernous area far down in the lowest level of the building, a kind of dark void where enormous room-sized rolls of paper for the company's printing presses were stacked in great brown palisades. We discovered this area in the course of wandering around killing time; deep within it, strangely, we found a soda machine and a picnic table with chairs and a burning light bulb overhead. I've always wondered why such things were there; we never saw anyone else in the area. Nobody ever seemed to use the machine or the table and chairs but us. It was like a set for some arty European movie. Sometimes we'd stay there for hours, joking about what was happening or not happening above ground in officeland, talking about movies and books and whatnot. Nobody ever seemed to miss us upstairs—the bosses themselves had almost nothing to do, remember, and probably were disinclined to get curious about disappearing subordinates—and there never was anybody downstairs to notice us.

All of us were gone from that company within a year. All left voluntarily. I was the first to go, and I departed on the assumption that I'd simply been extraordinarily unlucky in my first grown-up job. I assumed that Meredith had to be an aberration, that wherever I went I was bound to find more to do and more interesting things to do and people who didn't have to stupefy themselves to keep coming back every day. And on the whole I did find things better elsewhere. Not as much better as I had hoped, but better. On the whole I found that the smaller the organization, the better things tend to be. I found what working men and women have been finding for more than a century now: that big bureaucracies are a form of death in life wherever you find them, whether they belong to some corporation or to some branch of the government.

What happened at Meredith Publishing Company after my friends and I quit? Did bolder and more imaginative people take the places we'd vacated? Did they seize the opportunity we'd missed and stimulate a wealth-creating orgy of creativity in the staid shelter-publishing industry? Not that I ever heard. Some of the living dead who were there when I left are still there twenty-five years later, some in pretty much the same jobs, some a good deal higher up. What I know doesn't suggest that the ones who rose were more alive, more creative, more human than the ones who didn't. It's not impossible that my old boss is still there in the same chair, the same pencil in hand, staring at the same blank piece of paper.

In my days of lightning and thunder I was proud of having left Meredith when I did for the reasons I did. I was proud of that for the same reason I was proud of having majored in English in college instead of in engineering or business administration or some other safe thing. Now, of course, I'm up against the fact that if I'd been a good lad and stayed faithfully in my cubicle and said Death to Irony I would probably be safely employed today. Things would be delivered to my in-basket every morning. I'd have paid vacations and a pension to look forward to and maybe, by now, a parking place with my name on it. If I had young subordinates and they disappeared for long periods every morning and afternoon, I would be careful not to notice.

The same part of me that wishes it had gone to law school wishes it had stayed at Meredith Publishing. The part that was for so many years proud of having said to hell with law school, to hell with Meredith, is now trembling in a corner, curled up with its hands over its head.

During World War II, after my parents were married, my father worked in defense plants and made better money than he would have thought possible five years earlier. He and my mother bought quality furniture for their four-room apartment, one of those railroad flats where you had to pass through the bedroom on your way from the living room to the kitchen. They bought a new car. In their photos from those days my father wears a snap-brim fedora, my mother smart hats and high heels. They look like they've stepped out of one of the *Thin Man* movies.

As the war drew to a close the defense plants started shutting down. There was still a lot of money in circulation, plenty of work available, but if you were inclined to worry there was also plenty to worry about. As things turned out, of course, the people who bet on continued prosperity tended to do well in the fifties and sixties. My parents weren't the betting kind. My father went into the post office, a safe haven no matter what happened and a job to be envied if things turned really bad. If things got a little tight my mother took temporary jobs in offices and worked her comp-tometer. The years rolled by and things never did turn really bad again, and the post office looked less and less enviable, less worth the cost, with every new year. He stayed with it anyway, working nights first as a door-to-door television salesman and then in fur-niture sales, inching toward his pension. He never made a secret of how much he hated it, and along the way he began to drink too much.

Toward the end of my first year of college, in serious need of money, I myself took the test to become a trainee postal clerk. I hired on shortly after finishing finals. It wasn't officially a summer job; supposedly, I was starting a career. And it was good money for a kid: like all beginners I was on the night shift, and though I was paid by the hour I was often able to work twelve hours a night. When I was transferred to the parcels department the work became almost fun. Instead of sitting for hours on a stool, putting letters into pigeonholes, I was able to stay on my feet and throw parcels onto big conveyor belts.

One day the old man told me that a friend at work had asked him what he'd do if I decided to stay at the post office instead of returning to school. "I said I'd break both your legs," he said, joking and not joking.

Not that I would have considered doing any such thing. I saw my father mirrored again and again in the people I worked with at the post office: people living on automatic pilot, sorting the mail hour after hour and talking about baseball and women and about pensions that were so far in the distance they seemed to me to be somewhere in the vicinity of the planet Jupiter. The whole thing smelled of death. When September rolled around I handed in my official federal resignation form and went back to school. And across the thirty years since then all I've needed to do to make myself feel good about myself is think about life at the post office.

Today I sit at home all day and wait uneasily for the mail—uneasily because in the job-hunting game good news always comes by telephone. When the mailman shows up I think of the guys I worked with back in the parcel post department. Some of them are probably retired by now. The ones who aren't retired have the job security of manhole covers.

The part of me that should have gone to law school and should have stayed at Meredith considers sulkily that even the guys at the post office have had the last laugh.

The part of me that fled the idea of law school and never seriously entertained the idea of staying at the post office or at Meredith Publishing looks up scornfully from where it's been hunched over in its corner.

"Good Christ," it says. "You gotta be kidding."

Am I kidding? Damned if I know.

30

I GET CURIOUS about D, who lost a job as a corporate vice president nearly a year ago. I've heard nothing of or from him in months, and I wonder if he's had any luck or has learned anything that I ought to know.

I reach him at his vacation house up north. No, he hasn't had any luck. Nor does he have any leads.

He tells me that he's stopped looking. That he's fed up with headhunters who won't return his calls and with interviewers who—when he can get them to interview him—don't know what they're talking about. Not long ago, he says, he was in competition for a big job in New York with a man he knew from personal experience to be incompetent. Losing that one convinced him he will never again be offered a corporate spot.

He and his wife have put both the vacation house and their regulation suburban house on the market, he says. As soon as they can find buyers they're going to load their furniture into a truck and drive to the small town in the Carolinas where the wife grew up. D doesn't have any idea what they'll do when they get there. But the cost of living is low there, and he expects to figure something out eventually.

"I've been saving like mad for years," he says. "I'd hoped to be able to retire before I was fifty-five anyway. So it happened a little early. So big deal. I'll find a way to manage."

His words reinforce this sense I have that something is shutting down permanently in America, coming to an end. That what a lot of us have to look forward to is not a return to what we used to think of as normal but something new, a world in which lots of us who used to live in big houses in the best suburbs are going to be holed up, like D, in the woods.

Not a tragedy, necessarily. We're going to need a lot more information before deciding that this definitely is a tragedy.

PART III

Spring 1992

Too Soon Old, Too Late Smart

THE FIRST OF the mallards and Canada geese have made their appearance in Wisconsin: spring. And I have fewer job prospects than I had last summer.

A birthday has passed, so that I'm now one year older and have that much less value on the executive meat market. My professional credentials, so called, grow just a little staler with every passing month.

And with every passing month the burden of anxiety grows just a little heavier and feels a little more like something permanent. I spend increasingly big blocks of time daydreaming about what I might do if another six months go by and I'm still on the street.

I could go to truck-driver school and learn to operate one of those huge tractor-trailer rigs. There must be a living wage in it or there couldn't be so many. I could start wearing a feed cap and Levi's (far from a bad thing; Thoreau's advice was to "beware of all enterprises that require new clothes") and learn to talk with a trace of a drawl. I could pull vast loads from coast to coast and back again. Maybe buy my own diesel eventually.

Years ago a pal of mine, a bored-blind junior advertising executive at Meredith Publishing, answered an ad run by an over-the-road hauler looking for new drivers. The application form, when it arrived, was mainly focused on information about past arrests and convictions.

I've never been arrested. If that's all it takes, maybe truck driving is the career for me.

Or maybe my neighbor Jim would give me a job in the little air-filter factory he runs. Why not? He's constantly complaining about how impossible it is to find minimally competent and dependable people. I'm minimally competent. I'm capable of being conscientious. A year's take-home pay probably wouldn't cover a lot more than the taxes on my house, but it would be better than no job at all. And it could make me a local legend: the former briefcase carrier who spent the last twenty years of his life inserting tab A into slot B seventeen times a minute forty hours a week.

For that matter, I could try the last-ditch defense of the 1990s: something behind the counter at McDonald's or Burger King or Kentucky Fried Chicken. I would wear a little paper hat and dread the thought of having to wait on somebody who knew me when.

My favorite daydream is a classic American fantasy: I sign everything over to Pam, take a few thousand dollars out of the bank to tide me over until I connect somewhere, fill our old station wagon with as much personal gear as it will hold, get behind the wheel, and just . . go. Westward, of course. Just follow the highway to God knows where and start over from scratch and find out what a new life can bring. I could just as easily work at the McDonald's in Laramie, Wyoming, as at the one near home—just as easily, and with a lot less embarrassment.

One of Napoleon's illegitimate sons ended up as a short-order cook in the American West. What the hell: why not me? And why not Wyoming? It's so much easier for daydreams to take amazing turns when you set them in faraway places. My neighborhood McDonald's is a highly tangible reality, and its realness kills my ability even to imagine that it could possibly lead to anything. But I don't know anything about Wyoming. In Wyoming, for all I know, a job at McDonald's might lead somehow to a chance to write obituaries for the Laramie *Lariot* or whatever they call their rag. Twenty-five years later I'm the Rupert Murdoch of the Far West, sporting a Stetson as I arrive at Heathrow to begin my rescue of the London *Times*.

In another daydream I simply stop looking for work and stop having my hair cut and stop going anywhere or doing anything that could possibly involve the unnecessary expenditure of fifty cents. I never buy a new piece of clothing, never again own a car, turn my yard into a vegetable garden and my kitchen into a canning factory. Slowly I evolve into the crazy old man of Racine, Wisconsin, as my house falls in around my ears.

When I'm truly old and the last of my money is gone, I use a real-looking toy pistol and enter upon a career of armed robbery. If I succeed, banditry gives me the means to continue my eccentric existence. If I'm shot to death fleeing the scene of a crime, so be it. If I'm caught, no tragedy: I'll be put in a place where there's a warm, dry bed and free food every day.

A friend of mine, a woman in her fifties, recently quit her job as a writer for a giant corporation. She was trying to hang on for the sake of a pension and medical insurance but finally had to accept the fact that doing so was beyond her powers. Even her psychiatrist was urging her to quit. She tells me she knows she did the right thing but is more worried than ever about how she's going to live when she's old. I tell her about my armed robbery daydream. In her version of that dream, she replies, when she becomes old and destitute and unable to help herself she simply walks out into the middle of a busy street and lies down. "I figure *somebody* will have to do something about me," she says. Not necessarily, Marge. Not these days. All you can reasonably expect these days is that they'll drag you over to the curb so you're not a problem for the traffic.

But armed robbery—what a great idea! Every year they build more refuges for unsuccessful robbers. It's a top priority for the Republicans, in fact.

Failed robbers, unlike failed stockbrokers or artists or p.r. people, never need fear starvation.

32

Suddenly my reveries are interrupted by the surfacing of a vacant job. Whale ho!

An Iowa company called Pioneer Hi-Bred International, the world's leading producer of seed corn and such, is looking for someone more or less like me. Somebody who knows I'm on the street gives my name to the company's headhunter, Greg Carrott, who then calls me. Networking bingo. We meet in Carrott's Chicago office, and I take him through the usual highly sanitized and vastly edifying version of my life story, a version in which someone with my name is constantly and purposefully pressing forward from challenge to challenge and triumph to triumph. Carrott in turn tells me the usual things about how his clients are looking for a team player and a real strategist and all the things that all the companies say when they're looking for high-priced hired hands these days. It's like performing a ritual folk dance—something choreographed by somebody whose name everybody forgot long, long ago.

My time at J. I. Case has made me, luckily, a certified veteran of the agriculture business. Case isn't a seed company, but it builds machines that planted seeds and harvested the results. That's close enough to separate me from the city slickers, evidently. It also seems to help that I once lived in Des Moines, where Pioneer has its headquarters. As I'm leaving his office Carrott says casually that the fit between me and this job seems "almost too good to be true." The words seem momentous—seem written on the sky. Inside me the gray coals of hope suddenly turn orange. Suddenly I'm dreaming dreams of liberation.

Soon I get word that Pioneer is sending a delegation of three people to Chicago to meet with me. Not just with me, sad to say, but with me and three or four other candidates. Carrott says, however, that I'm the one with the broadest background and the most impressive experience. Again his words spread out against the sky. Little flames begin to dance on the glowing coals of hope.

It's been obvious from the start that if I get this job it won't exactly enhance my résumé. It carries the title of director, no small step down from the high plains where I've been feeding these past ten years. I don't much care about this, but there's no denying that it would be a further blotch on my already tarnished job history. What's far worse is that my willingness to consider it could easily prove a problem for Pioneer itself. Corporations and their headhunters are inclined to be suspicious of anyone willing to descend. Even today, amidst the layoffs and the downsizing and the unprecedented executive unemployment, they persist in wondering what's wrong with somebody willing to take a downward step. I'm quite ready for such a step, and Carrott seems to understand. As for Pioneer—there's no way of knowing.

Though little has been said about salary, I'd probably have to move lower on that ladder too. Again I'm perfectly willing, but they're likely to wonder why.

I tell myself that the simplicity of life in Iowa could be balm for my troubled soul. That if Pioneer doesn't appear to be a particularly interesting kind of company, neither is it a malignant kind of company.

As for stepping down in title and pay and size of staff and prestige and all the rest . . .

Surely I, of all people, am above such petty considerations. What I really want and need and deserve at this stage in my life is a chance to do simple, honest work for a simple, honest company in a simple, honest place.

Surely.

Throw a job my way—throw almost any job into my path—and within minutes I will explain why it is the one job for which my entire personal history has been a gradual but perfect preparation. The prospect of working for Pioneer Hi-Bred sharpens my devotion to simplicity and honesty to such a point that for the first time in my life I start going to a tanning salon. One of the how-to-find-a-job books says that to compete effectively for an executive position in today's America it is necessary to

(a) make yourself seem the sort of person who is far too busy and hardworking to have a tan, and

(b) have a deep tan all the same.

So every day for a while, then every other day, I go to the local salon and pay for the privilege of stripping down to my shorts and inserting myself into a kind of baking oven that within two and a half weeks has me looking like a homely George Hamilton or, more accurately, like an H. L. Mencken dipped in café au lait. If this is what it takes to get a job, so be it. I'm willing to do a lot more than this to get a job.

I go into training as if I were a fighter getting ready for the match of his life, an over-the-hill right fielder trying to pull himself together for one last spring training. Boxer-like, I even increase my roadwork, adding miles to the jogging regimen I've been following for years.

I collect information about Pioneer. I come home from the library with an armload of books on the history of agriculture and the mysteries of corn growing and the issues facing tillers of the soil all around the world.

While I'm doing these things, other jobs start popping to the surface. Résumés mailed out months ago suddenly bear fruit. A headhunter calls from New York and asks if I might be interested in looking into the vacant vice presidency of an insurance company called The Principal Financial Group, which is also head-quartered, oddly enough, in Des Moines.

I read in a newsletter that the U.S. Catholic Conference, the Washington-based policy arm of the Catholic Church in America, is looking for a director of media relations. I, as it happens, am the kind of Catholic who takes an interest in religious issues. Handling media relations for the U.S. Catholic Conference could, for someone like me, be interesting. Permanent escape. I imagine myself working in a cubicle instead of an office, wearing a checked shirt and hush puppies to work, shedding my "executive" identity like a snakeskin. I put a résumé in the mail.

A headhunter calls from Connecticut to say he's looking for a head of communications for Consolidated Edison, New York City's electric utility. Not long afterward, when his travels bring him to Chicago, we have a breakfast meeting. Then his partner passes through Chicago, and I have breakfast with him too. Both men convey the impression that before long I'm likely to be invited to meet with Con Ed's CEO in Manhattan.

So many things popping up suddenly, and every one of them apparently a real possibility. All of them together creating a tangled web of questions.

The Des Moines–based Principal Financial Group is, like Pioneer, a relatively obscure operation, attracting little if any attention in the world at large. And it's an insurance company. A friend who has done a good deal of work with insurance companies says the operative term for virtually all of them is "brain-dead."

But The Principal (I quickly school myself to capitalize the article in the reverential style used in all the company's publications) is strong and healthy and old-fashioned. Once hired, I'm told, people there are never fired. That's nothing to sneer at. And it's reasonable to hope that the soporific qualities of Des Moines might be exactly what my whole family needs after the turmoil of these past several years.

No doubt about it. Pioneer and The Principal are exactly what I've been looking for.

But if that's so, how can I be genuinely interested in Con Ed? Its headquarters aren't merely in New York but in Manhattan—the heart of the heart of the beast. And Con Ed, as a utility, would embroil me in an endless round of conflicts and controversies: electricity rates, pollution, the whole extravaganza. All in the center of the wildest media circus on earth.

How could someone who hungers for Iowa also hunger for that?

Without a trace of difficulty, actually. Con Ed could put me back in the big time—big salary, big staff, big budgets, big everything.

I always liked being in the big time. I have no problem persuading myself that Con Ed is exactly what I've been looking for.

But if Con Ed is exactly what I've been looking for, how could I possibly be interested in the U.S. Catholic Conference?

Again, no problem. The U.S. Catholic Conference could, I think, offer me work that I really would find worth doing. No corporation has ever really done that. In return, of course, I would receive an income that I no longer know how to live on.

But I can learn! I can accept the idea of never again ordering a bespoke suit—of maybe never again buying a suit of any kind. I can imagine myself commuting to work by bicycle, never taking a vacation more exotic than fishing in the Smokies.

I can do that! If what I get in return is liberation from bullshit, I ought to be able to do it quite happily.

And what of my "family responsibilities"? Hey, everybody in my family is a grown-up now. Let them get their own jobs. If they want to ride something better than a bicycle, let them get their own *good* jobs.

On a small piece of paper I make a list:

Pioneer.

U.S. Catholic Conference.

Principal Financial Group.

Con Ed.

And—my newest nibble—Dun & Bradstreet.

I pin the list to the bulletin board above my desk. My eyes come to rest on it whenever I look up.

I meditate on my little list. I tell myself that I couldn't possibly lose out on all of these. Couldn't *possibly*. Not on *all* of them.

When the time comes for my meeting with the delegation from Pioneer I am tanned and fit and brimming with facts about corn.

I am ready!

33

J, WHO HAS BEEN my friend since before we roomed together in college, gave up on trying to be a stockbroker back in the recession of the early seventies. He went back to school and had himself retooled as an information-systems specialist. A computer nerd.

For quite a few years now J has been a senior information-systems manager with the Federal Reserve. Computers, the Federal Reserve . . . I'd have trouble thinking of something that sounded more secure.

Today I got a letter from J. The Fed is consolidating, reducing head count, downsizing. J's boss, after thirty years, has been let go. J's boss's boss has been let go. J himself says he figures he'll probably be safe for another year, won't be safe at all after that. He's looking for tips on how to look for a job and figures I ought to be an expert by now.

It's getting harder and harder to find somebody to envy out there.

34

THEY'VE SEATED ME on one side of a long narrow table in a brilliantly white, brilliantly modern room twenty-five stories above the Chicago Loop. It's a corner room, two of the walls glass from ceiling to floor. When I look across the table, past the people sitting opposite, I see one of the world's great displays of skyscraper architecture. Turning my head, I can look out and down upon a Lake Michigan that extends to the horizon and is startlingly blue in the sunshine.

Everything here—the plush furnishings and gleaming appointments, the tall wooden doors, the chimney-like thick-bottomed water glasses, the silver decanter—everything is expensive, elegant. Everything says Money. Power.

This is the big time, the super-high-rent suite of offices occupied by the Chicago staff of Egon Zehnder International, one of the truly global executive search firms. And these are merely Egon Zehnder's Chicago offices—merely a satellite operation. The firm has its world headquarters in Zurich, its U.S. headquarters in Manhattan, outposts like this one in many places. It can be assumed that all of them are occupied, as this one is, by platoons of MBAs in gold cufflinks and Hermès ties and stiffly starched white shirts.

And remember that Egon Zehnder is merely one of the global search firms. One of many, and by no means the biggest.

It's an industry, this headhunting thing. It has grown up out of nowhere, one of the many strange things that have taken root and flourished in the peculiar soil of today's business world, and every year it pulls in fees that add up to hundreds of millions of dollars. One of the strangest things about it is the fact that, for all its size, most people barely know it exists. It produces nothing, not even ideas. Its sole purpose is to spare the world's most powerful corporations the indignity of having to find their own candidates for some of the most coveted jobs on earth.

The more you think about this, the odder it seems. The more you learn about the headhunting trade, the more it seems designed to multiply the costs and complexities of finding and hiring senior managers while narrowing the choices of everyone but the headhunters themselves.

As my mother asked in connection with separation packages: why do they *do* that? Why do many of the biggest corporations, which have huge resources staffs of their own, pay so much for the services of so many recruiters? Recently I got—not an answer, exactly, but a clue that seems to point in the direction of an answer. I called a woman headhunter named Jean Cardwell, an independent operator who specializes in p.r. jobs. I didn't expect that she'd have anything for me—most of her searches seem to involve lower-level jobs—but I was hoping that she might be able to give me some leads. I've been acquainted with her for years, and I know lots of people who know her well. I know she makes it her business to know what's happening everywhere.

"Well, gee, I don't know," she said when I told her what I was looking for. "Actually there *are* a couple of pretty juicy new searches just getting under way. But you know, Jerry, when you were working you never gave me any business. I've got to think first of the people who thought of me."

Oh, I thought. Now I get it. Now I see how the game is played. I hire you now. Later, when I get into trouble, you help me find a job. I should have been able to figure that out on my own. Too soon old and too late smart.

Anyway, here I am seated at this handsome table in this splendid room in the offices of Egon Zehnder International. Pioneer Hi-Bred has retained Egon Zehnder to protract and complicate the process of finding a new director of communications—not even a very exalted job. Somewhere off to my left, out of my line of sight, is Greg Carrott, the Egon Zehnder headhunter handling the search. For his troubles he will receive a fee equaling half the new director's annual salary or more. Plus repayment of his considerable expenses, of course. Today he will be only a silent witness to the proceedings. Later, probably, it will be his duty to tell his clients what to think about what they have just seen.

On the other side of the table, facing me, are two members of the delegation sent by Pioneer Hi-Bred International to Chicago. One is a silver-haired, seemingly mild and friendly man—a specialist in finance, a senior vice president, the eminence to whom the new director of communications will, once hired, report. At his side is a dark, attractive woman, also seemingly pleasant, of early middle age. I'm not sure what her role is; she has some vague administrative title that I couldn't have repeated ten seconds after we were introduced.

The two of them—the man, mostly, but the woman too from time to time—are lobbing easy questions at me. I am, I think, hitting them back cleanly one by one. They're asking about my background, my business experience, my thinking on management and communications and all the usual stuff. They probe in gentle, Iowa-polite ways to see if I know anything about agriculture; my preparatory studies come in handy here. They ask what I would do if confronted with this or that kind of little problem (every problem they pose is a little one).

I remember the things I've been told about how important it is to seem cheerful, interested, enthusiastic. I remind myself to sit forward in my chair and be positive. I keep up a smiley face and watch for opportunities to say something amusing.

Wouldn't it be wonderful, I think, to be an auto mechanic, say. And to be interviewed by other mechanics—people capable of judging whether you know your trade and determined to find out. Or to be a cook interviewed by other competent cooks. Or a p.r. guy, for that matter, under scrutiny by a panel of experienced and competent p.r. people. It's only when you're a mechanic being interviewed by cooks—a p.r. guy being interviewed by whatever these people are—that things start turning to bullshit on you. It's only in the realm of bullshit that the main worry is whether you're looking happy and interesting and eager.

Anyway, on we go. Am I a team player? What are my thoughts on corporate cultural change? From time to time, so that she won't think I'm intentionally excluding her, I turn to my right and address a few words in the direction of Pioneer's third representative, a woman who has seated herself on my side of the table but far down at its end, at the corner. She's a plump little character, with dumpling chins and the arms of the Pillsbury Doughboy. Her dress, a gray-and-white affair extravagantly adorned with laces and ribbons and frills, combines with her spherical, soft flesh to create a maternal, almost a grandmotherly, effect.

Except for her crew cut. Her graying hair is cut nearly down to the scalp on the sides of her head and is at most an inch long at the top. I recognize this as the current fashion; even Pam has a similar cut, though not nearly so extreme. But on this woman, draped as she is in all these doilies, a crew cut throws everything off-key. This is a woman whose parts don't fit together.

Carrott had told me days before that one of the people I'd be meeting, one of the women, would be a former clinical psychologist now on Pioneer's Human Resources staff. He'd gone on to say—I had let it pass without asking what he meant, unfortunately—that I might find her questions "unusual." This crew-cut woman has to be the one. Though I haven't yet heard any of her questions, I definitely find *her* unusual.

For nearly an hour she has said nothing. I continue to throw her a glance from time to time, and every time I do so she's a little more hunched over in her chair, staring at me a little more intently. Eventually she's bent over so far that if I hadn't seen her standing when I entered the room I'd suppose that she must be deformed. Her chins are nearly touching the table. The end of the ballpoint pen she grips so ferociously is nearly in her nostril. Her stare has become a glare.

As her expression and posture become more bizarre, I turn over in my mind (with the interview bubbling along) the fact that she's a trained psychologist. It's impossible to believe that someone as peculiar as she appears to be would be sent out on presumably important interviews. Suddenly—voilà!—it occurs to me that if she can't be as peculiar as she seems she must be behaving this way for a reason. That maybe I'm being subjected to some sort of test. Maybe the Pioneer people want to see how I'll react when confronted with something absolutely bizarre.

But even if this is a test—a risky thing to assume, obviously—what kind of response are they looking for? Should I do exactly what I am in fact doing—continue with the interview as if nothing odd were going on at all? Or will they decide that there's something wrong with me if I don't seem aware of the behavior of the woman at the end of the table?

But what could I possibly be expected to say?

"Excuse me, ma'am—is there some problem?"

Could I look to the others and say: "Do you think maybe we ought to call a doctor?"

I shove all such thoughts aside and try to fix my attention to the questions I'm being asked and my answers. It won't stay there, though.

Might *that* be why all the questions I'm being asked are so dull—because they're nothing more than background, of no actual importance at all? Am I being fed empty questions so I can't use my absorption in them as an excuse for not seeing, not reacting to, what's happening just a few feet away? If this is a test, could it possibly be such a complicated one?

Is it a test?

With a great act of will, I shove such thoughts aside.

As we get into the second hour of the interview the crew-cut woman straightens a bit and asks a question at last. And immediately a new problem arises: I don't understand what she's asking. I can hear her words, but they're so convoluted I literally have almost no idea what they mean. I apologize, tentatively feed her words back to her in a new sequence that makes some sense to me, and ask as politely as I can if this is what she means. When she assents to my second or third rephrasing I spin off some words that seem to be—that I fervently hope are—relevant in some way to whatever it is she wants to know.

"Is that responsive to your question?" I ask. She gives a grudging little nod. Then she hunches down again, makes more notes, puts her glare back on me, and the others resume their questions.

This happens again and then again. Each time the woman speaks, she stumps me. I go back to wondering about a test. I wonder if perhaps I'm flunking badly by not pinning her down, not being more insistent—but with impeccable delicacy, of course—that she make herself clear.

But I honestly am *trying* to get her to be clear. I can see no way to go further in that direction without crossing the borders of rudeness. None of the guides has recommended rudeness as a productive interview technique for eager seekers of work.

Perhaps an hour and twenty minutes after the start of the interview, the man and woman across the table start gathering their papers together, fussing the way people do when they're ready to bring things to an end. Their words take on the old wrapping-things-up tone: "Well, this has been very enjoyable . . ." In the midst of these little ceremonies the crew-cut woman uncoils herself, sits erect with her hands folded on the table in front of her, takes command.

"Let me ask you something," she says in a prim, school-mistressy way. "Suppose you have just come to work for Pioneer. And suppose we're the members of your staff, and this meeting that we've just had was our first staff meeting. What exactly would you have concluded about us on the basis of what you've seen?"

Jesus H. Christ.

"Um," I reply. "Let me be certain that I understand you here. You want *me* to tell *you* what I *think* of you. On the basis of this interview . . . "

"That's right. Judging from what you've seen, what do you think you'd have to do to manage us?"

Christ. A test for sure. A *trap* for sure. Nothing this odd could happen in this kind of situation by accident. But still, the right answer is not obvious. Do I tell her she appears to be one extraordinarily unusual woman? That she and her colleagues don't seem to be capable of steering an interview into subject areas that matter?

I don't think so.

"Well," I say finally, "on the basis of one short talk I don't think I can draw many conclusions about you at all. Nothing beyond the fact that you appear to be intelligent, well-intentioned, capable people. I certainly haven't seen anything that would give rise to particular concerns. Nothing, certainly, that would point to serious problems."

"Well then," says the woman with the crew cut, "let me ask you about me specifically, then. What would you say, on the basis of what you've seen here today, about me? And about what would be involved in managing me?"

"Welllll . . . " I draw the word out while my mind races. Do I dare to say that what I've seen has made me wonder if there's something seriously wrong with her? Do I dare *not* to say something of the kind?

"Let me be sure I'm clear on this," I say, stalling for time to think. "You want me to tell you what I think of *you specifically* as a result of this afternoon's meeting."

"That's right." She nods with satisfaction. Again I remember that she's a psychologist of some kind. I don't know what to do with that fact, exactly. But it seems to increase the likelihood that some sort of game—not necessarily a deep game, but a complicated one for sure—is being played here.

"Welllll . . . I guess I would say, on the basis of what I've seen, that you strike me as a very *analytical* kind of person."

Analytical! Good word! How did I come up with it? As soon as it's out of my mouth I'm delighted with it. I don't know myself what it means in this context—nearly anything, potentially—but I don't see how anyone could possibly object to being called "analytical." If it doesn't mean anything, all the better! Perfect, in fact!

And so I continue:

"I would tend to assume that, if I'm right about your being an analytical kind of person, you probably like to see things dealt with in very clear terms. Spelled out clearly. Naturally I'd want to try to work with you on that basis."

Evidently the woman lacks the wit to ask me what I mean when I call her analytical, or why I think that's what she is, or why I would try to be more precise with her than with other people. Any such question would skewer me.

Evidently she doesn't know I'm bluffing. Therefore she can't call my bluff. Still, she will not shut up.

"What does your conclusion suggest to you about me in relation to the others?" she asks and gestures at the man and woman on the other side of the table. They gaze back at us blankly. "What does it suggest about how you might manage my relationship with them?"

Enough. Enough of this crazy woman. She's got me out on a limb, and it's pure blind luck that she hasn't yet sawed the limb off. As far as I can tell she doesn't possess a saw. Can't count on that, though. Got to crawl back to safety.

"My conclusion doesn't suggest anything about that," I say. "I haven't seen nearly enough to get any ideas about how to manage your relationships. Even assuming that my conclusion is correct, which it isn't necessarily. I'm sorry. I just don't judge people that quickly."

I mean what I'm saying. But when I listen to myself saying it, I seem to sound like a prig. An evasive prig.

Minutes later, as headhunter Greg Carrott is walking me out to the elevator, I ask him how he thinks things went. On the whole he seems positive. It was a good session, he says, except for "a little interview fatigue toward the end."

The elevator doors close on me before I start wondering who it was who looked fatigued.

The woman with the crew cut? Or me?

35

An hour later, replaying the interview in my head, I feel myself going glum. Going into a low-grade depression, really, feeling that what I need is to find a dark place where I can lie down and suck my thumb for a while.

Probably a letdown is to be expected after a long-awaited, protracted, important interview. It doesn't necessarily mean that the interview was a disaster. Not necessarily.

Remembering this doesn't exactly lift my spirits, but it helps me keep my balance.

After a few more hours depression gives way to resentment. Then, in stages, resentment turns to anger. What kind of interview *was* that? What kind of *people* are those, that they'd put me through such a thing? What the hell kind of *company* would send out such people on such a mission? Who could possibly want to *work* for such a company?

I remember how, in trying to get ready for the interview, I'd imagined myself a boxer training. The fight is over now, and it wasn't anything like what I'd expected. The other fighter had been dressed in a clown suit, and all the hard punches had landed below the belt. And there had been no referee.

And whatever the judges' decision eventually turns out to be, there will be no possible way of understanding it. Even if I win on points, I'm not likely ever to know how or why.

What kind of process *is* this?

I'd also imagined myself a ballplayer given one brief last chance in the batting cage. Well, my chance came and now it's gone. Most of the pitches were served up underhand, so that a child could have hit them. All the hard ones were in the dirt.

Nothing was proved, nothing was learned. There wasn't even an umpire on hand to call balls and strikes. Just a pitcher in a clown suit throwing the ball into the dirt while a little crowd of bystanders looked on in silence.

A farce.

If I'd ever been drawn into such an interview while securely in a job, I'd have withdrawn from contention before leaving the room. Now, though, I'm not secure about anything, and there's nothing to do but let my anger burn down. I concentrate on the hope that I'll be invited to the Pioneer headquarters in Des Moines, and that on its home ground the company will look less . . . screwy.

Greg Carrott is better than most headhunters at sharing information. (When I thank him for this, he tells me he once had a mentor who told him to remember that they weren't in the business of playing games with people's lives. All headhunters should have such a mentor.) Before long he calls to tell me that of the four people interviewed, one had been a complete flop, had "bombed out completely." I hold my breath and wonder if he's talking about me. He goes on to say that the other three had all done well—had in fact been described by the silver-haired senior vice president as "a Mercedes, a BMW, and a Cadillac." I continue to hold my breath. Finally he says I'm one of the automobiles, and that I am, therefore, now one of three surviving contenders.

I don't have the nerve to ask if I was the Mercedes, the BMW, or the Cadillac. I do, however, want to see if I can learn something about the fat woman with the crew cut. I want to know if it's necessary to keep worrying about her.

"That was a . . . an unusual interview," I say. "An *interesting* interview. That one woman, the one who sat off by herself . . . was she *trying* to throw me off stride? Was she playing some sort of . . . game? Testing my reactions, maybe?"

Carrott speaks slowly in responding, apparently being careful in choosing his words. "No. Not really. I guess I really don't know *what* to say about her. I do think she *means* well . . ."

So. Pretty clearly it had not been a trick interview, hadn't been designed as a trap. It was nothing more complicated than a strange woman being allowed to play a disruptive, destructive part in an interview that was—for me, anyway—a hugely serious thing.

Learning this does not make me feel better. I feel anger flare up again, anger mixed with more of the kinds of questions for which there doesn't seem to be an answer.

Why have I ended up being interviewed—being judged, presumably—by a crazy woman?

How can a crazy woman have a job when I don't?

How could a crazy woman be allowed to help decide whether I'm going to GET a job?

What's going ON here?

The next time Carrott calls, it's to tell me the field is now down to two finalists. I'm one of the two. I'm either a Mercedes or a BMW, evidently.

"I assume this means I'll be invited to Des Moines before long," I say. "For more interviews. I and the other contender."

"In any normal situation I'd say that that definitely should come next," Carrott answers. "But this isn't a normal situation. I think this is a situation in which some internal candidate—some star salesman, somebody out of the law department, someone completely unexpected—could be brought in out of nowhere and given the job."

"In other words, they don't know what they're doing."

"You got it."

36

THE ARCANE strategies of the desperate job hunter . . .

Dave, still working the phones harder than anyone I know and still not getting any interviews, takes a break when I drop in at outplacement. He tells me, laughing about it, that he recently read some interesting advice on how to improve your odds of getting noticed when you answer a job ad:

1. When you find an ad that interests you, cut it out of the paper.

2. Put the ad on your windowsill.

3. When the ad has turned yellow, answer it.

The thinking behind this is actually not bad. Ads for attractive jobs, as I know well from the days when I was doing the hiring, often draw great stacks of mail.

Going through all that mail is not fun. It invariably turns out that most of the applicants aren't what you're looking for at all. Doing the reading necessary to figure this out rapidly gets tiresome. After a while even the letters and résumés of the applicants who *are* qualified all start to look pretty much the same. That's tiresome, too. Whoever has to go through all this stuff gradually gets exhausted, confused, disgusted.

You, meanwhile, haven't even written yet. You're still waiting for the ad to ripen on your sill.

And when you finally do write, long after all the others, your letter upon arrival looks like something fresh and new and delightful. It looks like an excuse for your prospective boss never to have to look again at those festering piles of old mail.

You've rescued him. You're in. Bingo.

I honestly do think it could work.

37

THE END COMES with merciful speed but otherwise is not surprising. Pioneer doesn't hire me or any of the others interviewed that day high above Lake Michigan. They also don't give the job to an insider. Somewhere and very quickly they find a new candidate who satisfies their expectations, whatever those may be, and hire her.

Fair enough. My biggest regret is that I hadn't dropped out the afternoon of my interview.

Within days of getting the word from Pioneer I receive a letter from the U.S. Catholic Conference. They've selected six finalists to be interviewed, and I'm not one of them. Apparently there are plenty of Catholics out there who have good media-relations credentials, are hungry for low-paying work, and can do a better job than I with questions about Church issues. Fair enough, but obviously this is a *tough* job market.

One of the headhunters for Consolidated Edison calls to tell me that I'm no longer in contention there. Con Ed's CEO has instructed him—this is a secret, he warns—to find black candidates exclusively. They haven't found one yet, but they're looking. They're scouring the country. Fair enough. If blacks are getting a few extra breaks in the job market these days, I for one have no complaint.

I'm also out of the running at Dun & Bradstreet. Again the reason is a secret: the CEO has decreed that the job has to go to a woman. Again, fair enough. If women are being given an extra advantage here and there, that hardly seems an injustice after all the generations when they were given nothing at all.

Of all the companies on the list above my desk, the list that couldn't conceivably fail to generate a job offer, I am now down to a single remaining possibility: The Principal Financial Group, the other Des Moines company.

The people at The Principal appear to be very interested in me. They've spent considerable sums on getting me interviewed and evaluated and having my background and my references checked and doing all the other things a company does when a search is in process and there's no need for hurry and money is basically no object.

I know from talking with people who know the insurance business that The Principal is, even by the standards of its industry, an extraordinarily conservative company. This is a good thing insofar as it kept the company from speculating heavily in real estate and junk bonds in the eighties. Though it's far from being one of the country's biggest insurance firms, in the aftermath of the Reagan years it has emerged as one of the biggest insurance firms not in serious financial trouble. Another nice thing is the way The Principal's conservatism (or wisdom, or timidity, depending upon your angle of vision) translates into a kind of old-fashioned paternalism. The word "fired" has never been part of the company's vocabulary. At one time I might have laughed at such a consideration; never again.

The negative side of all this conservatism and paternalism is that The Principal almost never hires outsiders except at the entry level. It depends in every possible instance—which means that it nearly always depends—on promotion from within. Now they've decided, obviously with excruciating reluctance, that they have no choice but to go outside to find a successor for the communications vice president who will soon be retiring. Or that they *probably* will do so. That they *presumably* will. Assuming that doing so continues to seem necessary.

As The Principal puts one hurdle after another in my path and I jump them one by one, I begin to think that this is what it would be like to attempt the seduction of a forty-year-old virgin. She wants to do it. She *really* wants to do it. But when you bring her to the point of decision . . . well, it's *such* a big step. And if we don't do it today we can always do it tomorrow. If we go ahead and do it today, on the other hand, we can never undo it. There's no going back. And no need to rush things.

The Principal's headhunter, a New Yorker named Jim Wills, passed through Chicago and met with me over dinner. He said he was looking at scores of candidates—literally at scores—and hoped to give the company a list of about half a dozen names representing a spectrum of different backgrounds and skills.

In the next month he called me twice. First to tell me that I was on his shortlist. Then to say that I had been promoted from his shortlist to the company's.

The month after that two of the company's executives flew out from Des Moines and spent four hours questioning me. They seemed to be decent sorts—Iowa wholesome again, and Iowa cautious. Like their counterparts at Pioneer, they clearly knew almost nothing about communications. I didn't learn much from them or about them in the course of our talk, and I didn't see how they could have learned much about me. I was grateful, though, that they didn't have a crew-cut woman dressed in lace with them.

Now yet another month has gone by, and at last Wills has called to arrange for me to visit Des Moines. It will be a two-day visit, and it will include time with the CEO. And they want me soon. It sounds serious.

My visit is to be on a Monday and Tuesday. The company sends me tickets that will put me on an early-morning flight from O'Hare to Des Moines. I go to the library and see if I can find any articles about the company. There aren't any. I find some on the insurance industry in general, along with a couple of books on the same subject. These prove to be even less interesting than I'd expected.

I feel confident. Semi-confident, anyway. A little over three years ago I was offered the top p.r. job, a vice presidency, at The Travelers Insurance in Connecticut. Though I declined that offer—those were better times, and I was not yet damaged merchandise—I've made sure that the people at The Principal know about it. The Travelers is vastly bigger than The Principal, vastly more visible, faced with vastly more complicated problems. What I want

The Principal's leaders to think is that if I was good enough for The Travelers, I just might be good enough for them.

More than nearly anyone else I know, I am a good sleeper. Jogging helps make me so; it drains off so much physical and nervous energy that I rarely remain awake more than three minutes after putting my head on a pillow. One thing has always made it hard for me to get to sleep, though: the fear of not getting enough sleep when doing so really matters. This used to drive me half crazy when I was in college, working at outside jobs, helping to put out a weekly paper, and trying in the midst of everything else to cram for finals. Halfway through an exam period, after getting a total of perhaps nine or ten hours of sleep over three nights, I'd find myself going to bed desperately tired but also desperately aware of how much worse things were going to be the next day (another exam to take, followed by the need to get ready for yet another one) if I didn't fall asleep *soon*. Needless to say, I would not fall asleep soon or at all. By the day of my last exam little green men would be dancing in front of my eyes.

In the hours before my departure for Des Moines, and for the first time in years, I fall into the old bind. And though I find a solution, it turns out to be at least as bad as—and in the end a good deal worse than—the original problem.

On Sunday, the day before the start of my trip, I go for an especially long run so that I'll be especially relaxed when it's time to sleep. Before ten that night I drink a cup of warm milk, get into bed, open the less-than-fascinating new biography of Woodrow Wilson that's been my bedtime reading for weeks now, and wait for the nodding-off to start as usual after a few pages.

Before the first nod, though, Pam comes running up the stairs. According to the television a freakish spring blizzard has struck to the south of us in Illinois. O'Hare is in chaos—flights canceled, people stranded by the hundreds. I leap out of bed. It takes me an hour of waiting on the phone to find out that the departure time for my flight has already been postponed indefinitely, with cancellation possible. In another half hour I have a new reservation on a flight out of Milwaukee and have managed to reach my designated contact at The Principal and tell him of the change. By the time I go back to bed every part of my nervous system is on red alert. I try to lose myself in Woodrow Wilson but can't think about anything but the blizzard and whether I'm going to be able to get out of Milwaukee in the morning and how in hell I'm going to cope with a full day of interviews if I don't get to sleep soon.

I turn out the light, try to fall asleep, realize after a while that it isn't going to happen. Eventually, I creep to the bathroom and surreptitiously, embarrassedly, sneak one of the little (and now rather old) red-and-white sleeping pills that a doctor once prescribed for jet lag but never actually tried. This is the first sleeping pill of my life; I don't know how they work and don't want to ask because I don't want a debate about whether I should take one. An hour later, still no closer to sleep and more desperate than ever, I take a second pill. Not long after that I am sound asleep. When the alarm goes off very early in the morning the skies over Wisconsin are clear. I reach the Milwaukee airport with time to spare, my flight takes off on schedule, and I arrive in Des Moines without difficulty.

There is a problem, though—a problem very difficult to describe. The person who has arrived in Des Moines somehow doesn't quite seem to be me.

Somehow everything is wrong this morning—and wrong in a way that's utterly unfamiliar to me. My mind, my perceptions, my whole system seem to be—I'm not even sure what word to use—seem to be *refracted*, perhaps. Yes: refracted. Everything has been thrown slightly but disorientingly off center by whatever was in those little red-and-white pills. It's not that I feel bad really. I simply don't feel that I'm *here* somehow. I don't feel connected in the usual way to the things I'm experiencing. My experiences don't seem to be mine.

Hour after hour that day I'm led from office to office and meeting to meeting, and none of it ever feels entirely real. I seem to be able—I think I am able, I hope I am able—to move normally and smile normally and answer questions and ask questions in a solidly normal way. I tell the people who interview me about how I once lived in Des Moines, worked at Meredith Publishing, worked for the *Register* and *Tribune*. I make a big deal of how much Pam and I loved Des Moines, how the first little house we ever owned was in the Beaverdale district, how I taught part-time at Drake while she finished her degree there, blah blah blah. I tell little stories about fishing in the reservoir just outside of town and about not being able to find Methodist Hospital the morning Ellen was born. I'm trying to get these people to think of me as one of them.

As each meeting ends, I have alarmingly little memory of what's just been said. It's the same that night, when an executive vice president takes me to dinner and wants to know all about the day's meetings and what I think about what I've seen. I have to struggle to find things to tell him.

I feel as if I've sent a deputy on a mission to a strange place, have received only the most disappointingly sketchy reports, and now am expected to describe the mission in detail.

What happened today? How the hell should I know? Ask somebody who was THERE!

The dinner with the executive vice president does not feel good. I wish I could tell him about the pills, about how they could be the reason why we seem to be boring each other so badly this evening. I want to tell him that these are the only pills I've ever taken, and that there's usually a little more to me than what he's seeing now.

Great idea, right? Tell the grandfatherly executive vice president of possibly the most conservative corporation in North America that things would be going better if only I hadn't been *taking drugs*. Great way to get a job.

That night I sleep well (without further chemical assistance, needless to say), but though I feel more like myself on Tuesday morning part of me is still in some fourth or fifth dimension, some distant cosmos where two plus two makes three point eight or four point one.

How long does this damn stuff last?

The day starts with a long meeting with the CEO. He too is curious about yesterday's meetings, and again I try to conceal the trouble I'm having remembering even the names of the people I'd met. The CEO seems a nice enough man. He also seems dry, narrow, dull.

Is it the chemicals that make me think so?

I'm put in a car and taken on a tour of Des Moines. People have been telling me proudly how much Des Moines has grown, how much is going on here. To me, today, despite all my genuinely good memories of the place, it seems the dreariest town of its size I've ever seen. The downtown, which supposedly has been booming for nearly twenty years, looks comatose. The suburbs are exactly how Gertrude Stein would have pictured the suburbs of Des Moines: a flat and barren expanse of mud and clapboard, clapboard and mud. No *there* there.

The chemicals again?

When everyone is finished with me I have hours to kill before my flight. The weather has turned steamy warm, so I set out on a walk. I circle through the downtown area. It's as much a blank from the sidewalk as it had been from the car—nothing of interest, nothing happening, not a single shop I'd like to browse in. After a few blocks I find myself—amazing thing!—outside the headquarters of Pioneer Hi-Bred International. I walk into the reception area and look around. Everything is very modern, very swank. What if the crazy woman walks by, I wonder. Would she recognize me? If she recognized me, what would she say? What on earth would *I* say? That I just happened to be in the neighborhood? I get out of there as quickly as I can.

I start to feel hungry, and the most inviting place I can find for a sandwich in all of downtown Des Moines is the lunchroom at the YMCA. I look in at the library, then at the police headquarters where I once worked so eagerly as a young reporter. Then, because there doesn't seem to be anything more to look at downtown and it's still too early for the airport, I set out for the neighborhood that years ago everyone regarded as the best in town. South of Grand, it's called; Pam and I and most of our friends in newspapering and teaching thought of it as the place where the upper crust lived. If we were to move to Des Moines now, it's where we would look first for a house. Twenty minutes of fast walking get me there, and when I arrive I see it hasn't changed at all. It's what I remember. But somehow, without changing and without deterioration, it has diminished. It's exactly what I expected and at the same time it disappoints. What comes to mind as I walk the streets on this warm and humid afternoon with plants of every description starting to push up out of the ground, what I keep thinking of is—mildew.

MILDEW? This has to be the chemicals, still messing with my head.

The walk back to my suitcase takes me along a street of little storefront insurance agencies and TV repair shops and plumbing-equipment wholesalers.

As I trudge on I go through the usual exercise of trying to replay the interviews, trying to remember who said what and how it felt at the time. I try to figure out whether they went well, and if so how, and why. This time it's harder than usual, obviously.

I become aware of how urgently I'm *hoping* that everything went well—how desperately I want these people to have liked me and been impressed by me.

In a similar situation in a different culture I would sacrifice a ram on the steps of The Principal's headquarters, said to be the tallest building between Chicago and the Coast. I would prostrate myself in the spilt blood and pray for deliverance.

I hope I hope I hope I hope I hope . . .

Then, in the midst of all this fervent aspiration, a simple question pops startlingly to the surface of my mind:

Why?

Why have I got my whole existence centered on this thing?

Because I need a job, obviously. Because if The Principal doesn't offer me a job I'm going to have to keep repeating this process until somebody does. Or until I'm no longer allowed to repeat the process, or have become incapable of doing so.

Because I've lost control of my own life and don't know how to get it back except by seducing somebody into hiring me.

At that point other new things come pop, pop, popping up— not questions this time, but discoveries. Realizations. On a sterile commercial street on the fringes of downtown Des Moines a con-fused and discouraged middle-aged man has an epiphany.

Suddenly he sees clearly that he really, *really* doesn't want to live in this place.

That he really has no interest in The Principal Financial Group, either—hasn't yet seen a single way in which working there could possibly be interesting, or absorbing, or fun.

That at bottom he doesn't give a damn whether the people at The Principal like him or not.

That the extent to which he's been obsessed with such things is a measure of the extent to which he's surrendered control of his own life.

And that there *has* to be a better way of regaining control than this.

He stops and looks around at the blank windows of the low storefront buildings and the gravel parking lots and the big empty sky, and he knows one other thing for sure too:

This time it's not the chemicals talking.

This time it's real.

38

ON THE FLIGHT home from Iowa I compose a letter telling the headhunter Jim Wills that I no longer want to be considered for the job with The Principal Financial Group. By way of explanation I say that even after my two-day visit I still don't understand what the company is looking for. I say further that I can find no way of judging whether I would like the job, or do well in it, if it were offered to me and I accepted. Whether, over the long term, management would be happy with me even if in my own opinion I was doing the job well.

It's intended to be a polite way of saying that they haven't shown me anything. Of saying thanks but no thanks.

That night I run the letter through my word processor and seal it up for mailing. But in the morning I don't mail it. I can't. It's exactly the letter I would send if I were safely in a job instead of being desperately in need of one. If other people weren't so dependent on my getting back to work. But how could I possibly explain to Pam that though as far as I can tell the interviews in Des Moines went well enough—hadn't been a calamity, certainly—I'm dropping out? That though this is a strong and profitable company, and though its leaders clearly are at least somewhat serious about the possibility of offering me work, and though I don't have a single other live prospect just now, I've decided to call the discussions off. How could I defend such an act?

I couldn't, obviously. After all these months of doing everything possible to find a job and not getting a single offer, after seeing more and more people lose their jobs and have no more luck than I'm having in finding new ones, after growing more and more accustomed to seeing beggars on the streets of every city I visit, I cannot throw this chance away. Even though the job's attractions are strictly negative—an escape from fear, from insecurity, perhaps from having my whole family go bust—turning my back on it would be pure bravado. And pure bravado, these days, carries a higher price than I can afford to pay.

I tell myself to grow up, that dramatic gestures are for children. That it's still far from clear that The Principal is going to make me an offer, and that while they're making up their minds I can continue to look elsewhere. That it's not inconceivable that something better will come along very soon. Not at all inconceivable—merely extremely improbable.

If I'm offered the job and take it and it turns out to be as boring as I expect . . . well, hell, I've had boring jobs before. That's why they call it *work*. When I start feeling bored I'll have no trouble remembering how lucky I am to have a job. I'm not good at slogging through day after day of tedium, at pretending to care about things that don't interest me, but I've proved that I can do it.

So I write the usual thank-you notes and once again settle in to wait. And the wait, as usual, proves to be a long one. I hear nothing in the days after my return from Des Moines. But that's okay. This kind of silence doesn't distress me in the same way it did six months ago. In fact it adds almost nothing significant to the dull background ache of loss and rejection and fear that has become a familiar companion. I've grown accustomed to chronic low-grade emotional pain in exactly the same way I probably could get used to hemorrhoids or a broken kneecap. The fact that I no longer really believe that this waiting is going to end with a job offer cuts the tension considerably. Near-hopelessness isn't fun, but it helps in keeping anxiety at tolerable levels.

Eventually Wills does call. Among the candidates the company has examined, he says, I'm now the sole survivor. It's an ambiguous honor for sure, but the only kind of honor currently available. Wills says they now have an inside candidate they want to consider, however, and that's going to take time.

I want to ask how it's possible for an inside candidate to emerge this late in the process. But I don't. I want to say, The hell with it, tell 'em I ain't interested anymore, but of course I don't.

A few more weeks go by and Wills calls again. He's a little vague in what he has to say this time, but he conveys the impression that I'm still the leading candidate, that the inside candidate has been tested and found wanting. Now another outside candidate has emerged, however. Nothing can happen until this new prospect has been seen and checked out. My mind blossoms with questions, the biggest of which is the question of whether these people are going to keep digging up new candidates until they finally succeed in locating one who doesn't trouble them in the way I, apparently, do. If that's so, I'm twice a fool not to drop out now. Wills's vagueness appears intentional, however, and so once again I swallow my questions.

On a Friday afternoon, after another two or three weeks of silence, Wills calls yet again. The Principal's decision-makers (or non-decision-makers, more accurately) have told him they now have everything they need. Next week most of them will be traveling, but the week after that they'll all be in Des Moines. They intend and expect to make their decision during the week after next.

"So I'm still in contention?"

"Oh, very definitely. Very, very definitely."

That sounds good.

"Have any questions come up in the process of talking with my references, verifying my background—any of that?"

"Not at all. Everything's tracking exactly as you'd expect—exactly as it should."

That sounds good, too.

"But I have to tell you," Wills continues, "it's entirely possible that the final decision is going to be to do nothing at all."

"Not make me or anybody else an offer, you mean."

"That's right."

"After all this."

"Right."

Half a year ago this kind of thing would have sent me into seizures of anger, anxiety, and resentment. Now it mostly just disgusts me, makes me feel tired. Once again I wish I could just tell them all to go away and leave me alone.

But everything will be decided by the end of the week after next, Wills had said. Within ten working days at most. Even if the process runs true to form and takes twice as long as predicted, we're still only talking about twenty working days. That's nothing compared with what's already behind me. It's now something like four months since I had dinner with Wills and he first told me about the job. It's ten months since I started looking for a job. Ten or even twenty more days of only slightly embittered uncertainty are nothing, absolutely nothing, compared with that. I'm reminded of the soul in Purgatory in an old George Carlin routine: "Only two aeons to go! Hey, I could do an aeon standing on my head!"

Hey, I can do a month standing on my head.

Or so I like to think. In actuality the promise of a decision soon throws me back into a familiar mode: trying not to think about the fact that in a faraway place people who don't really know me are deciding the rest of my life. Of course I think about it almost constantly. Though I am telling myself I don't really care, I care more every minute.

I read somewhere once about a White Bear Club. To qualify for membership you have to go stand in a corner and for fifteen minutes not think once about a white bear. Anyone capable of that would do well in my present situation. Other human beings, normal ones, should avoid this situation if they can.

Late on Monday afternoon, at the end of the first day of the week when nothing can possibly happen, I tear a long narrow strip from the edge of a sheet of yellow legal paper. I tape one end of this strip to the bottom edge of a picture frame across the room from my desk. It hangs there like a ribbon, like some award I've given myself for getting through a whole day of final-phase waiting. On Tuesday afternoon I do the same thing. And on Wednesday. When the week is finally over five shreds of paper hang from my picture frame like a row of military decorations, one for every twenty-four hours of agony endured. It pleases me to look at them. They represent the only kind of achievement that seems to be within my grasp these days.

And so ends the easy part—the week when there was sure to be no decision and therefore silence can't possibly have some terrible hidden meaning. The next five ribbons—assuming that as many as five will be needed—are going to come a lot harder. But they ought to finish the job.

The next five ribbons do indeed come harder. The second Monday seems endless. But it does end at last (I could do a Monday standing on my head!) and a sixth yellow strip goes up. I consider it proudly. Then Tuesday: another endless day, ending at last with a seventh yellow ribbon.

And questions rumble around like bowling balls inside my head.

What's going on in Des Moines? Have they met? Why haven't I heard? If something about me has them worried, why the hell don't they call me in so we can talk about it? Shouldn't they take another look at me before making a decision? Wouldn't that make sense?

Of course it would make sense, screams the inner voice that used to be a mocking one and now is raving mad. *Of course it would make sense! That's why there's absolutely no chance that anything of the kind will happen! Haven't you been at this long enough to have figured that out by now?*

Mercifully, the voice falls silent. The parts of me that are still more or less sane, still capable of more or less adult behavior, note with satisfaction that the picture frame across the room looks as though it's growing a yellow beard.

That's what passes for progress around here these days.

S LIVES ON our street. He came to Wisconsin from Pennsylvania less than a year ago with his wife and two daughters to become head of marketing for a company here. In Pennsylvania, he's told me, he was downsized by a failing company and spent most of his savings before landing a new job at last.

His first assignment in Racine was to make big improvements in the department he'd been hired to run. In the process of doing this he got rid of and replaced a big part of his staff. He didn't like doing it, he says, but he could see the need.

Several weeks ago, satisfied at last with the quality of his staff and satisfied therefore that the bloodbath was at an end, he took his family on a skiing vacation. He returned home to discover that he, too, had been fired. The first clue came when he arrived at his office early on Monday and discovered that the phone had been disconnected. "The chemistry just wasn't right," his boss explained. He now suspects that the company had this whole scenario in mind when he was hired. They needed someone like him to do a job that no one else had the stomach for, he thinks. And as soon as the job was done—Adiós!

They offered him one month's separation pay. He hired a lawyer whose intercession got that doubled. Now that I know what the job market is like I know what a bad deal that is.

Yesterday I happened to notice that a great many high branches had been trimmed from a huge tree in S's side yard. The mere thought of doing such a thing made me dizzy.

"It needed doing and I decided I'd better do it now," S explained. "My health insurance expires at the end of the week."

TEN FULL MONTHS without work now, and the end of my separation-benefits package is coming into view.

Human eggs fertilized the day I was fired are bawling babies now. And I have nothing to hope for aside from word from The Principal Financial Group. Which is to say that I have very little to hope for.

It's time for something new.

Time for something that never fails to seem exciting and fun when you read about it in magazine articles or hear motivational speakers tell inspiring stories about how it can work. And never fails to look pretty nasty when you drag it out into the light of day and give it a close look.

I need to see if I can find a new way to make a living.

Ridiculous amounts of paper are being expended these days on articles about the new (and always wonderfully exciting) challenges that face America's white-collar workforce, and about the things (also wonderfully exciting) that happen when displaced executives muster the courage to strike out in new directions. Sometimes it seems impossible to pick up a business magazine without finding still another article about the wonders and excitements waiting for those of us who are strong enough and imaginative enough to shed our neurotic attachment to concepts as obsolete as jobs and embrace new ways of working and living.

The relevance of such ideas to people in my situation is all too obvious. The fascination of such ideas for all the people who fear falling into my situation is likewise all too understandable. We wouldn't be seeing all these articles if people by the millions hadn't demonstrated an eagerness to read them. There wouldn't be nearly so many seminars on how to put your life on a new and better path if the people who make their livings thinking up subjects for seminars hadn't discovered that Americans in great numbers will pay for the privilege of attending.

But a common and pretty basic flaw runs through all this stuff. It fails, I think, to take into account some of the realities of everyday human life, and some of the most basic needs of normal, ordinary human beings.

For example, a good many self-proclaimed organizational gurus have been writing and lecturing about how the corporation of the not-very-distant future will have only a tiny, almost vestigial permanent staff. This corporation will meet most of its needs for white-collar work by hiring outsiders temporarily, project by project, inviting them to come aboard long enough to complete some specific, limited task and then inviting them to go away again. Most of the kinds of people who until now have had conventional salaried jobs will become a new class of migratory brain workers, moving into and out of assignments as opportunities ebb and flow. Their lives—*our* lives—will become a jumble of brief encounters.

If you're careful in choosing the words to describe this scenario, it can sound like a grand adventure. Corporate bureaucrats are transformed into *consultants*. Middle managers become *freelancers*. Everyone *goes where the action is,* and plain old-fashioned work is replaced by *innovation* and *empowerment* and *total quality* and *adventure*. The man in the gray flannel suit, like a caterpillar turning into a butterfly, is transmogrified into a soldier of fortune.

But the people who describe this future never seem to wonder what kind of society it's going to be when many of us are skittering not merely from assignment to assignment but from job to job and company to company and, presumably, city to city.

I haven't yet heard any of the gurus explain what we're supposed to do, where we're supposed to go, *between* our wonderfully exciting assignments. Or how we're supposed to get to an assignment in Los Angeles when we're in Baltimore and haven't had an assignment in eight months and therefore are flat broke.

Does anyone expect that the people in this kind of world are going to be capable of building or sustaining communities?

Of even knowing what community is?

Of raising families?

What are we supposed to do about health care? About feeding ourselves when we're too old for wonderful adventures? About disabled kids or disabled parents? About *any* of the problems for which there are no solutions in this swashbuckling country of ours if you don't have either a secure long-term job with some solid organization or a fat inheritance?

Peter Drucker, probably the smartest and most credible business prophet around, says the society of the future is going to be the most competitive in history. I wonder: is that a fit society for the mass of human beings? Are most people *made* for that kind of society? Is it going to be wonderful—or constant misery on a global scale?

There are answers to some of the problems caused by the changes we're experiencing, of course. We could have a health insurance system that didn't leave millions of people permanently vulnerable to instant ruin—something on the European model, maybe. We could have portable pension systems, so that if people are forced to live like gypsies they won't easily be doomed to destitution. But such answers are politically infeasible in America, evidently. What drives me nuts is the fact that they can't happen because the same big interests that are busily pushing millions of people out of the traditional job system are absolutely opposed to letting such changes happen. It's dog eat dog out there, and as usual the big dogs are winning.

Do they have to have *all* the bones?

Peel away the uplifting rhetoric about the exciting workplace of the future and what you're left with is an America in which stability, continuity, and security—the basic elements of a coherent life—are going to be beyond the grasp of all but an increasingly small, increasingly isolated minority.

Across the whole country we'll see a kind of endless session of musical chairs, with fewer and fewer safe places, a shrinking cluster of frightened survivors struggling more and more ferociously to stay in the game, and a steadily growing crowd of losers looking on sullenly from the sidelines.

I agree with the experts about one thing. It's going to be *exciting*. We really do seem to be in the middle (or at the beginning, for all I know) of one of the most profound social transformations since the start of the industrial age. The earth is moving under our feet, and everything is up for grabs. The chances that the results are going to turn out to be good for most people, though, look pretty small to me. What's most likely ahead, I'd guess, is something much more like a vast jungle than any kind of community.

Another thing the experts say is that, in the world that's now being born, job skills will have the life span of fruit flies. They say—the exact numbers vary a bit from one guru to the next, but the general point is always the same—that from now on we're going to have to be prepared to change jobs eight, ten, or twelve times in the course of our working lives. And all of us will change *careers* three times or more.

Hey, I'm all for it. Seriously, I think it could be delightful. When you consider how thankless so many jobs turn out to be, how empty most so-called careers, the idea of making a significant change every four or five years and a really drastic change every ten years or so can be downright delicious.

But when you try to *do* it—and lately I've been looking hard for ways to do it, driven by the fear that if I don't find a new career I might find myself with no career at all—things get pretty complicated pretty quickly. It doesn't take long before you find yourself wondering whether the idea of regular career changes makes a shred more sense than the idea of sending the whole country off on an endless round-robin of temporary consulting assignments. You don't have to spend a great deal of time looking into it before you start to wonder whether, in an economy as ramshackle and flyblown as ours, such a thing is even possible.

Mind you, I'm not talking about crazy pipe dreams. I'm not talking about resigning from the accounting department and going off to become a movie director. Or about leaving the phone company because what you always really wanted to be was a cabaret singer.

I'm not even talking about things like my end-of-the-tether fantasies—fantasies about giving up and heading west to start life over from scratch, or going to truck-driver school, or taking up a broom in the service of Colonel Sanders.

I'm talking about undertaking a sober self-analysis, a cold-eyed examination of what you know you're capable of doing, what kinds of jobs are available in the real world these days, and how the two things might be made to fit together.

I'm saying that it's possible to perform exactly that kind of analysis, conduct a systematic search for ways to make exactly the kind of career change the gurus are recommending, and find out that in today's world it may not even be an option.

PART IV

Summer 1992

Stenches

41

PAM'S DAD WAS, until he died, an agent for the Mutual Benefit Life Insurance Company. He was proud of the company; it had helped him climb into the suburban middle class with only a high school education. He believed fervently in the company's mission and made it his own mission. Pam and I hadn't been married very long when he showed me the payoff that could come with buying what were called "ordinary life" policies at an early age and then letting their value grow.

As the years passed and my income grew I bought more and more insurance, and it became increasingly clear that Pam's dad had been right. The cash value of our policies got to be significant. Whenever we chose, we could borrow from it at low interest. Over the long run, obviously, it was going to provide a lot of money for our retirement. Or, God forbid, for a rainy day.

It is now raining. And though I don't need my insurance money yet, I can easily imagine needing it eventually. It's even easier to imagine a point at which the premiums we pay each year are more than we can handle.

And, right on schedule, Mutual Benefit is now in mortal trouble. Long one of the country's genuine blue-chip insurers, during the go-go years it fell into the hands of people who invested its assets in ways that, when you hear about them, are nearly impossible to believe. In a horse farm, for example. Mutual Benefit's management actually put vast sums into *horses*. And lost every dime.

As a consequence, the company has now fallen into even more improbable hands: those of the New Jersey insurance commissioner. For a while there was some question of whether our tens of thousands of cash-value dollars might be gone forever. Now we've received word of a reorganization that's supposed to put things right. We still don't have access to our money, but a plan devised by New Jersey supposedly will prevent it from going down the drain. We are encouraged to expect that we will, eventually, be made whole. After nine years, to be precise. Provided that throughout those nine years we continue to pay our premiums.

You say you can't afford to do that? Tough.

I could scream. I could throw a bomb. I wonder aloud how much the geniuses who wrecked the company were paid while they did so. And how much they were paid for leaving when they went.

Pam says she is thankful her father didn't live to see the company he loved—love is not too strong a word for it—come to this.

42

ALL OF A SUDDEN I'm working. Sort of. In Chicago. Sort of. It's all so weird. Hip hip hooray.

It started with a call from a guy named Tom Amberg, whom I knew slightly years ago in St. Louis. He's now the president of a Chicago p.r. agency called Aaron D. Cushman & Associates. He called after I answered a Cushman ad (oh yeah, now that you mention it I think I remember that ad) for an account executive. When I answer ads of that kind these days, I do so more out a sense of duty than with any real hope of getting a response.

Tom asked me to come down to the Loop for lunch. At Shaw's Crab House he said that although I'm ridiculously overqualified to be an account exec (whatever you say, brother) he had something more appropriate in mind. Cushman's biggest client, Century 21 Real Estate, had recently demanded the replacement of the man who managed the account. Not because the man had done anything wrong or had failed to perform well, Tom said. It was just one of those chemistry things.

If I would sign on, Tom would make me a senior vice president. He named a salary that was exactly half of what I was still getting from J. I. Case.

The wheels in my head started turning:

The day I take a new job, no matter what it pays, Case is off the hook. My separation package still has a couple of months to run. Signing on with Cushman would be the same as throwing away something in the neighborhood of twenty thousand dollars.

Still. It was a job. And it was being offered to me.

I made a counterproposal: let me start working at the salary suggested, but for a while let me be a consultant instead of an employee. What's in it for you, for the agency, is that you won't have to provide me with benefits. I'll make out, you'll make out, and if everybody's happy a few months from now I'll go on the payroll for real.

Tom agreed immediately. I think he must have been under heavy pressure to get somebody on board fast. And so suddenly I'm *senior* vice president of an established agency in the heart of the City of Big Shoulders.

Oh, wow.

What this means, actually, is that I now spend five days a week hidden away in a small and dirty back office with peeling paint on the window frame, a desk that wouldn't bring twenty dollars at a garage sale, and sinister stains on the carpet. There are four grand spaces at Aaron D. Cushman & Associates: a reception area, a conference room, and the offices of Tom Amberg and Aaron D. Cushman himself (who has been vacationing in Florida since my arrival). These four spaces are up front, and they're the only spaces visitors are ever allowed to see. Behind them is a long corridor in which the rest of us toil obscurely like idiot offspring kept out of sight of the world.

What we toil at is the most utterly meaningless work I have ever done in my life. Whatever the client, the objective is always the same: get publicity. Get the client's name in the paper: any paper, any way you can. Exactly what I've never wanted to do.

Forty years after its founding, twenty years after passing its peak, the Cushman firm is down to its last high-paying client. Century 21. The one I've been recruited to manage. Most of the others—and there aren't that many—are not only small but shaky. Around the office I hear a lot of talk about whether this or that client is going to be able to pay its bill. My office, such as it is, is directly across the corridor from the business office. I hear a lot of hushed and urgent talk about what checks have come in and whether certain checks have cleared and where the balance sheet stands.

At first I tried commuting to Chicago from Racine. The morning trip involved a twenty-five-minute drive from home to the Kenosha train station, followed by an hour and twenty minutes on the train, followed by a walk to the office that took only fifteen minutes if I moved really briskly. In the evening it was the same thing in reverse. After two weeks of this I was catatonic. And so now I have a one-room efficiency in an old building in the Hyde Park neighborhood south of downtown. I stay there four nights a week. My bed pulls out from the wall and is five feet from the stove. After work I cook myself a pot of Rice-A-Roni, watch television for a while on a six-inch black-and-white screen, and go to sleep early. As often as not I'm awakened in the middle of the night by somebody leaning on a car horn or by drunks screaming at each other in the street.

When that happens I sit up in bed and watch the glow of the street lamps in my window. I wonder how in God's name it ever came to this.

But I am, don't forget, a *senior* vice president.

It's like being executive officer of a garbage scow.

43

It's impossible to accept Aaron D. Cushman & Associates as my destiny. The idea is intolerable. I'm going to—I have to—keep my eyes open for a real job.

I'm going to continue looking into possible new careers too. If teaching is out, there's still journalism. Journalism wouldn't require breaking into something new. All I'd have to do is pick up the threads of my own past.

Or so I think. It turns out there are no threads to pick up.

The editor of the *St. Louis Post-Dispatch,* where I'd once been something approaching a star reporter and had been selected for a fellowship program at Harvard, writes in reply to my inquiry that he has no hope of being able to hire anyone in the near term. He says he's been paring staff through attrition for over a year. The editor of the *Baltimore Sun,* whom I'd met when we were reporters on Nieman fellowships at Harvard, responds in exactly the same way. Are these people simply giving me a polite brush-off? It's entirely possible. But I still have friends at the *Post-Dispatch,* and they tell me the situation there is even grimmer than the editor's letter had suggested. The mood of the city room, as they describe it, makes me think I'm not missing a thing. Weeks after getting the letter from the *Sun's* editor I see an article about deep layoffs there.

I write to the *Chicago Tribune* and the *Milwaukee Journal* and definitely do get the brush-off. The director of the foundation that awarded me the Harvard fellowship twenty years ago, when I ask if he has any suggestions about how a former golden boy might possibly find a spot writing for a newspaper somewhere, sends back a plaintive reply. He says that it pains him to receive appeals like mine because he's receiving so many of them and can't do anything to help. He says he has a desk drawer filled with letters from able and experienced reporters, onetime stars many of them, who are out of work and unable to find work anywhere.

Journalism is another area, apparently, where the world has moved on and left me behind. So maybe I used to be a pretty good reporter. So big deal. There isn't much call for those anymore.

Probably everybody in my situation thinks at some point of starting or buying a small business. The lure is obvious: you become your own boss, you start reaping the benefits of your talent and hard work, you liberate yourself from at least some of the things that have been chafing your soul since first you became a wage slave. It's the American dream, the ideal way to make a living—unless in the process of doing it you lose every dollar you possess. The percentage of fledgling entrepreneurs who do in fact ultimately lose everything is high. Which is one reason why most people spend their lives working for other people even when they hate doing it.

I look at every week's fresh crop of Wonderful Franchising Opportunity ads in *The Wall Street Journal,* but I never see anything that makes me want to bet the farm. Most of them involve fast-food places, quickie oil-change joints, and printing and duplicating services. Many of them appeal explicitly to displaced executives: "Frustrated? Tired of giving everything you've got and getting nothing in return?" "Looking for a good place to land with your golden parachute?"

Like everyone else, probably, I know people who bought McDonald's franchises early and got very rich. But I know also that hundreds of people have lost their shirts on Roy Rogers franchises and Minnie Pearl franchises and God knows how many other get-poor-quick debacles. Among all the new franchise ideas now being pitched across America, it's entirely possible that one or two are going to make a lot of money for a few shrewd or lucky plungers. I'm equally sure that I have less chance of picking the winner than I'd have of finding the pea in a sidewalk shell game.

When I try to think of some kind of small business I might enjoy running and be capable of running, the only possibility that comes to mind is a small newspaper—a weekly published in a county seat somewhere, say. This is, of course, one of the most hackneyed clichés in the history of executive daydreams. But in my case, because I've been a writer and editor and manager, it does seem to have at least a shred of plausibility.

I've written to, and talked on the phone with, people who are supposedly among the country's leading newspaper brokers. I've described myself to them, told them far more than I'm accustomed to telling strangers about my financial status, explained my reasons for possibly being interested in buying and running a paper. I've asked if they think such a step might make sense for me. Oh my, yes, they say. They send me big envelopes crammed full of copies of newspapers currently for sale and information about them: circulation figures, local demographics, columns of numbers detailing income and expenses, columns supposedly showing how much the present owners are paying themselves in salary and how much remains as profit at the end of the year. The pages presenting these numbers are always signed by a certified public accountant, but under the signature there's always a disclaimer to the effect that the numbers are unaudited and the CPA is not affirming their accuracy.

Every time I get another packet of this stuff I study it carefully and respond quickly. I tell the brokers what I like about what they've sent me, what I dislike, where my uncertainties lie, and where I'd like more information. I always say that though it's improbable that I'll decide to buy any of the papers they've sent information about, I'm interested in working with them. I'd like them to help me learn about the newspaper market, I say, so that eventually I'll be capable of investing without excessive risk and with a reasonable chance of success. Not one of these brokers has ever responded. They're either a remarkably lazy breed or remarkably crafty. Either they don't want to work for their commissions or they want nothing to do with buyers who ask too many questions.

One of the envelopes sent by a broker contains information about a little weekly that's for sale in Hermann, Missouri. I know

Hermann. It's a picture-book little German town perched on wooded bluffs above the Missouri River between Kansas City and St. Louis. Immediately I start spinning fantasies about becoming the William Allen White of Hermann, being accepted by the good burghers because my name is Meyer, about writing wise and witty editorials and book and movie reviews for my little paper and going trout fishing twice a week. When I write back to the broker about this one I include an unusually long list of questions, and I don't include the usual statement about how I probably won't want to buy this particular property. When he doesn't write back I'm unusually disappointed.

Sometime later I happen to tune in to a public television documentary about the exporting of American jobs. As an example of our national calamity, the documentary focuses on a big Florsheim shoe factory that is being moved to Mexico. From Hermann, Missouri. No more jobs for Hermann. No more customers for the local merchants. No more ads in the local paper. Ruin for the local William Allen White.

Reluctantly I come to the conclusion that owning a small-town paper is a great idea for anyone who wants to work insanely hard for a microscopic salary and who, probably, will go broke in the long run.

Which is just as well, in light of the vehemence with which Pam has opposed the whole idea from the start. As the owner of a little paper, she says, I would sit at my desk and compose those wise and witty things, or try to. She, meanwhile, would find herself selling ads, negotiating with printers, dealing with accountants and lawyers and circulation headaches. She's right. I drop the subject.

So . . .

Where does all this leave me in terms of what the gurus call "reinventing" myself—boldly seizing control of my destiny and moving on to a new career?

Where it leaves me is exactly where everything seems to leave me these days: with questions for which I have no answers.

What new career?

Where?

Where the hell *are* all these alternative careers? I don't know anybody who's found one.

One of the things the gurus like to say is that we middle-aged American executives need to learn not to be so rigid. We need to be willing to accept change and adapt to it. Hell, I don't think I'm rigid—not in that way, anyhow. I think I'd be quite willing to make a career change, even a radical one, and could enjoy doing so.

But *where?*

How?

44

I AGREE TO spend an hour on the streets of downtown Chicago soliciting contributions for the Salvation Army.

En route to my assignment I see a guy walking along East Wacker Drive on the south side of the Chicago River, magnificent glass towers all around. He's trim, well-groomed, wearing a good suit. He's also wearing front-and-back sandwich boards that bear his name and phone number and a neatly printed message:

I am a graduate of UCLA. These are my credentials. I need a job in marketing.

At the corner of Wabash and Randolph, wearing a colorful little apron, I hold out a cylindrical container into which the people walking past on their way to work can put their donations. Many of them grimly ignore me; the effort to avoid my eyes gives them the look of zombies. Others give apologetic little smiles and keep on walking. Surprising numbers of people stop and dig in their purses and billfolds. Obviously it makes them feel good to do so. Seeing them feel so good makes me feel good, makes the whole morning seem to glow. I'm smiling the whole hour. I don't know how much money is in my cylinder when my time is up, but it's clearly a lot.

This is the best experience I've had in months.

There's a lesson in there somewhere.

45

IF I CAN'T GET full-time work as a teacher, if the kind of teaching I used to enjoy doesn't even exist anymore, maybe I can get into the academic world through a different door. I start answering ads run by colleges and universities looking for staff communications people, public relations people, publications people, whatever.

Once I start looking for them I find lots of such ads. In responding I always include not only a copy of my résumé but a long, thoughtful letter trying to demonstrate how my experience in business really could be useful in an academic setting. Always I emphasize my connection with academia—my graduate studies, my part-time teaching, my two years on a university board, whatever.

I must have sent at least a dozen such letters. Not once have I ever received more than a pro forma response—a polite but impersonal kiss-off, often in the form of a pre-printed postcard. "We have received your materials. Thank you for your interest. If we decide to contact you further you will hear from us by March 15. If you do not hear from us, be assured that we are sincerely grateful for your interest." Blah blah blah.

Not once have I been summoned to an interview. And I'm pretty sure I know why. It's because I'm coming out of a corporation. American business and the American academy—though you'll rarely hear anyone in an important position on either side say so publicly—loathe each other. Anyone who becomes identified with one camp will find it difficult at best ever to be accepted in the other.

Because at various times I've been in both camps, I've probably seen more of this mutual loathing than most people. I know what academics say about corporate executives when they're among themselves, and I know what executives say about academics. In my first job after the Navy, at Meredith Publishing, I worked with a man named Guy Neff. He was near retirement when I met him, had never risen very high in the company, and was now reporting to people who obviously didn't have his brains, talent, or sophistication, even a greenhorn could see it. Guy and I used to talk—he was the only older executive in that dull place who seemed able to sustain a conversation about anything beyond football and golf—and we got to be friends. He told me one day that the reason he hadn't done better at Meredith's was that he carried with him the "academic stench." He meant that he had a master's degree in English, that he'd been a teacher before going into publishing, and that even after joining the company he'd continued to teach evening classes. *The academic stench.* Because of it he never became one of the guys. And this was in publishing. In one of the macho fields his handicap would have been five times more crippling.

Years later a history teacher at my son's high school came to see me because he hoped to find a job in business and wanted advice on how to do it. He had a doctorate from a first-rate university, but he'd been part of the Ph.D. glut of the early seventies (the papers were full of stories about young Ph.D.s driving taxis in those days) and as a consequence had never been able to get on the college-teaching track. He gave me a copy of the résumé he'd paid some company a ridiculous fee to prepare for him. It gave prominent place, not surprisingly, to his doctorate and his two other degrees, one of them a bachelor's with high honors from the University of Chicago.

I gave the résumé to an executive-placement specialist I knew and asked for his advice. What he said brought back memories of Guy Neff. The résumé had to be rewritten. Completely. So as to conceal that Ph.D. Especially because the Ph.D. was in the humanities. Otherwise this guy had little chance of being interviewed, let alone of being hired, by any large corporation. Corporations simply didn't want to mess with doctors of history or English or philosophy.

There is also a corporate stench. If the self-styled macho men of the corporate world have a cartoon image of professional academics (and they do), the professoriate tends to have equally childish ideas about what it is to work in business—especially big business. If executives like to be contemptuously dismissive of academics, to think of them as irrelevant if not ridiculous, some academic people seem almost desperately eager to believe that to make a living in a large business organization is to be venal, loutish, brutish, corrupt. It's the old C. P. Snow thing about two cultures coexisting uncomfortably in a single society, and it's still profoundly true.

Similar fault lines can be found in other parts of the American workplace. The health care industry, for example, has been bursting with jobs. Check the help-wanted section of any Sunday paper, even in the most depressed cities, and you'll see column after column of ads run by hospitals and medical schools and health maintenance organizations and the like. And they're not only looking for nurses and doctors and therapists. They need everything—accountants, marketing specialists, human resource specialists, computer experts. They even need writers and editors and p.r. flaks. It's the one part of our economy that's a cornucopia of salaried jobs with benefits even today. It's also intensely incestuous. If you have the qualifications specified in one of these ads but haven't worked in the health care industry, your chances of getting an answer when you write are poor. Your chances of getting an interview are poorer still. Your chances of being offered a job are somewhere out near the vanishing point.

Maybe that's as it should be. For all I know, experienced people who have not worked in the health care field cannot adapt themselves to it. For all I know, many of these invisible barriers make good sense on a level so basic I can't even see it. Even if the barriers do make sense, though, their existence makes a travesty of all this easy talk about how we should all be ready to change careers and then change careers again. In my mind at least, it raises questions about whether the gurus know what they're talking about.

All I can say with certainty is that changing careers is much easier said than done.

"I THINK THEY were a little concerned that you were only with Case a couple of years. Not that they made a big deal of it. But I got the sense that it troubled them."

"Not much I could do about that."

"No, that's right. And I told them so. I told them that the average job tenure for p.r. people in New York is less than four years. By that standard you've been a paragon of stability, and I told them so. But I think it still bothered them."

Jim Wills, headhunter for The Principal Financial Group, is calling from New York to tell me that his clients have reached their decision at last. More than six months after starting their search, four months after I was first drawn into it, they've decided not to offer the job to me or to anyone else. Their plan is to let the search go dormant for a while, and then—or so Wills expects—start rounding up a fresh batch of candidates. Whether the search is ever resumed, I'm out of the running. For good.

"I think they got the impression that you're a very hands-on kind of guy," Wills continues. "Apparently that bothered them, too."

"Well, when you get down to it, I guess it's true. I guess I do tend to be a hands-on kind of guy."

I pause, disgusted with myself for repeating such an empty cliché despite not even being sure what it means. "But I guess I'd have to say I'm a little surprised to hear that it bothered them. I always thought being a hands-on kind of guy was supposed to be a good thing."

"Well," Wills says in obvious discomfort. "You know."

What it is he thinks I know I do not know.

47

Sᴀʀᴀʜ ʙʀᴇᴀᴋꜱ into tears as she tells Pam and me about her interview. She'd been preparing for weeks for a day of meetings with the people who run Teach for America, the new Peace Corps–like operation that sends young people to two-year tours of duty in some of the most needful school districts in America. She sat up late several nights running, preparing materials for use in a five-minute demonstration of her ideas about teaching.

Her main interview, she reports, was with a woman who kept looking at her watch and looking out the window and looking around the room. She asked questions in a bored tone, and she made it clear that she was exasperated by nearly everything Sarah had to say.

I tell Sarah that maybe the whole thing was a test of her ability to deal with the unexpected, with uncooperative pupils. On the other hand, I tell her, maybe the woman is just plain rude. I tell her about some of the interviews I've had.

I'm sorry, I say. That's just how it is these days. Welcome to our world.

IT'S PROBABLY at least a little ironic, in light of the extent to which the world of big corporations has taken over my life, that my few months at Meredith Publishing remained my only real exposure to that world until I was thirty years old and found myself, against my own wishes, assigned to the business news section at the *St. Louis Post-Dispatch*. The assignment filled me with chagrin. The sixties had just ended, and flower power was in full bloom. I, like many people my age at that time, thought of business as not merely uninteresting but unimportant—irrelevant. I wanted to cover politics. My highest dream was a spot in the Washington bureau. Instead I found myself being sent out to corporate annual meetings where nothing that anybody cared about was ever said (even the business editor agreed about that), and to corporate offices where I interviewed supposedly powerful men who usually seemed to be afraid of me because of what I might write. I soon decided that I hated interviewing big executives. The odd combination of their supposed power and their timidity—the care they took never to say anything that might possibly annoy anyone—made them seem the most colorless human beings on earth. Cabdrivers, welfare mothers, politicians at even the lowest levels of government—all seemed more human, more alive, than senior corporate executives.

I learned to take dullness and timidity for granted when dealing with corporations and their leaders, and therefore I wasn't at all surprised when I made my first visit to the biggest corporation in town and found it to be the dullest and most timid of all. My mission, when I called on McDonnell Douglas Corporation's headquarters, was to interview some senior executive on some subject other than the corporation itself. I can't remember the exact subject—something like trade policy or taxes, probably—or even whether I got a story out of the visit. What I do remember, and remember vividly, is how everybody there seemed aghast at the thought that a reporter was on the premises. The poor p.r. guy who escorted me was obviously petrified, and everywhere we went people were peering out at me fearfully from doorways and from around corners. When I returned their stares they would pull back as if shocked, as if I'd pointed a pistol in their direction. I was a lowly local reporter on a completely benign assignment, a skinny and slightly unkempt nobody with a steno notebook sticking out of the pocket of my thorny-looking old tweed jacket. But McDonnell Douglas made me feel like some fearsome invader from Mars, some angel of death. Back at my own office I used to joke about that visit, about how weird and pathetic McDonnell Douglas was.

There has been nothing stranger in my life than the fact that ten years after that visit my picture appeared in the *Post-Dispatch* along with the announcement that I had been promoted to vice president of—would anyone have believed it?—McDonnell Douglas Corporation. At which point I became McDonnell Douglas's youngest vice president.

A transition of such magnitude can only happen in stages. Stage one came three years or so after my first exposure to McDonnell Douglas. It was my decision—arguably the great mistake of my life—to accept a job offer from Fleishman-Hillard Incorporated, the biggest public relations agency in St. Louis.

Someone wiser than myself might have seen from the start that such a move could only end badly. I thought it was worth a try because I was thirty-three years old, was already beginning to find my reporting assignments repetitious, and had decided in the course of trying to see into the future that in St. Louis at least there appeared to be no such thing as a happy, productive, fulfilled middle-aged newspaper reporter. I loved being a reporter, loved writing long feature stories especially, but it seemed to be a young person's game. The reporters who were no longer young seemed to resent, and certainly scorned, the ones who were. They seemed uniformly cynical and sarcastic and worn-out. To me they looked like people whose hearts had been broken by their work. In keeping with legend, many of them drank too much.

My decision to leave became firm after I met with the managing editor and told him I was thinking about taking a job with Fleishman-Hillard. He said I shouldn't leave, that if I stayed there was no limit to what I could become. When I asked for specifics, he had nothing to point to. Apparently he expected me to risk my future on his willingness to do some unspecified good thing for me at some unspecified future time. This was a man who had never demonstrated the smallest real interest in my career—in my existence, for that matter. I thought the risk too great.

I could have tried another paper in a different city. Or maybe a magazine. But this was just a year after Pam's return to work. Moving out of town in the hope that my opportunities might be better elsewhere would be asking a lot of her. I thought it would be asking too much. The fact that Pam herself was vehemently opposed to my leaving journalism for p.r. made the whole situation even more complicated.

But I went into the p.r. business, and it took me nearly six months to figure out just how big a mistake I'd made. It was only after the simple relief that comes with changing old routines for new had begun to wear off that I started to miss the things that go with being a reporter: the freedom to be wherever things are happening, to bring shocking and heartbreaking and beautiful things to the attention of a whole city, to make captains of industry furious and poor old black women celebrities for a day.

Nor had I foreseen how much I would hate trying to get publicity for clients. After years of fancying myself a crusader, now I was being paid to get some banker's picture in the paper for doing something that I couldn't make myself believe was important or even interesting. Just making the effort was embarrassing. I'd been too lacking in self-awareness to realize that being the kind of reporter who gets to cover the big stories inflames the ego until it becomes as big and red as a baboon's butt. Now that I wasn't a reporter anymore, I found that some of my great and good friends didn't have much interest in me anymore. I could no longer help them, and I couldn't hurt them. I was no longer dangerous. I hadn't realized how many people were kissing up to me, or how much I enjoyed it. Now I could hardly believe how much I missed wielding the petty power of the press.

I hated the way all the businessmen I dealt with simply took it for granted that we were all good Nixonites together. I hated the way the big shots, now that they had no reason to fear me, seemed to take it for granted that I admired them. I hated the fact—an inevitable one, considering how much we charged per hour—that all our clients were fat cats. I hated the fact that one of the main things the fat cats paid us for was defending them against perfectly decent people (consumer advocates, ghetto people, leaders of ragtag worker groups) who usually had little money or power and would have had all my sympathy if I'd been a reporter covering their battles.

The things I hated were, unfortunately for me, the everyday realities of the agency business. Hundreds of capable and honorable men and women accept those realities every day without difficulty. I wasn't cut out for it somehow.

One day I looked across the cafeteria where I'd stopped for lunch and saw the managing editor of the *Post-Dispatch* sitting alone. I joined him at his table, and without much of a preamble I started telling him that I'd be grateful for a chance to get my old job back. This was not easy; the managing editor was not noted for his warmth. And I'm no extrovert—it's at least as hard for me as for the next guy to admit a mistake or ask for help. But here in front of me was the man who had urged me not to quit, who had told me that if I'd stay everything was possible. Here was the same man who had exclaimed, when I returned to his office and said I'd decided to take the Fleishman-Hillard offer, "I never thought you *meant* it!" So I plunged in. I asked.

He told me to get lost. Not literally; what he said, literally, was that there was a freeze on hiring (this was the early seventies, with a jumbo recession raging), and that he didn't know when the situation might change. But he said it so coldly, in so few words, that there was no doubting what he meant: get lost. I quickly did. I walked away feeling more thwarted than I'd ever felt in my life. But at the same time I was grateful that I hadn't stayed at the *P-D*. Disagreeable as my situation was, bruised as I was by such a curt rejection, I felt lucky not to have put my future in the hands of such a man.

I was still at the agency—increasingly miserable, unable to see a way out of simply quitting and hoping for the best—when an aircraft mechanic in Istanbul made a mistake that killed three hundred and forty-six people and changed the course of my life. A Turkish Airlines DC-10 went out of control shortly after taking off from Paris en route to London and plowed a swath through the Ermenonville forest in northern France. Every seat had been filled, and everyone on board died instantly. Very quickly it became clear that the crash had happened because a cargo door had blown off the airplane, causing rapid decompression in the cargo compartment, which in turn caused the floor of the passenger cabin to collapse. That in turn had severed all the control cables running from the cockpit to the tail. What wasn't known in the beginning was that the whole disastrous chain of events had been made possible by a maintenance error: a mechanic had disassembled the lock on the cargo door, and when he put it back together again he put the locking pin in backward. Until that became known there was no way of being certain that every DC-10 in the world wasn't a death trap.

The uproar was huge. Newspapers and broadcasters around the world demanded to know why the door had blown off, and why the loss of a mere door had led to the loss of the airplane. Travelers everywhere were suddenly afraid to board DC-10s, and across America some bona fide aviation-safety experts and a good many self-appointed experts were insisting on television that all DC-10s be grounded immediately. It was the worst disaster in the history of commercial aviation.

The DC-10, as it happened, was built by McDonnell Douglas Corporation. Within hours of the crash, as soon as the dimensions of the crisis became apparent, McDonnell Douglas chairman and founder James S. McDonnell called my boss at Fleishman-Hillard. He said he needed help in keeping the situation—in keeping the media, at least—from going completely out of control. My boss was a busy man who had no room in his schedule for a major new client but also, naturally, had no wish to turn a major new client away. So when he was called to a Thursday evening meeting at McDonnell Douglas he took me with him. At that meeting it was agreed that a news conference would have to be held as soon as possible. James McDonnell, a local legend known to all St. Louisans as Old Mac, decreed that this would happen on Monday in California, where the company's commercial aircraft were built. He decreed that Fleishman-Hillard would help with the preparations. What he wanted, undoubtedly, was the assistance of my boss. But my boss said he couldn't get free. And so on Friday afternoon I found myself on a plane bound for Los Angeles.

I spent all but a few hours of that weekend in the headquarters building of Douglas Aircraft Company in Long Beach, drafting and endlessly redrafting the speech that Douglas's president was to deliver at Monday's news conference. I would go over each new version with the president and a constantly changing group of engineers, and then on the basis of what they told me about where I had things wrong and what was being learned at the crash site I would do another version. For me it was a cram course in the rudiments of aviation technology. It was also an endurance test. Every time I finished a draft, a fresh platoon of experts would take it through another reading. They'd talk it through, debate technical things I had trouble understanding, explain where I'd gone wrong. When each session was finished, the experts were free to put their feet up, go off somewhere for a nap, even go home. But I had to return to my typewriter and start again. My Sunday dinner was a handful of jelly beans stolen from a bowl on somebody's desk. By late Sunday night I was nearly catatonic. But in the end we had a tight speech that seemed to cover everything and satisfy everyone. And I'd been completely won over by the people I was working with. It was clear that what they wanted was to tell the truth about their airplane, not to hide anything or distort anything or try to improve on the truth. And they seemed grateful for whatever I'd been able to contribute. These were professionals of a caliber I'd rarely encountered.

Monday's news conference was a kind of circus from hell, with big-time print and broadcast reporters on hand from around the world. I'd never seen so many celebrities from the fourth estate assembled in one place: people whose bylines I'd been reading with envy and admiration for years, familiar faces from the network news. Everybody there seemed eager to show how much he knew about airplanes, how wise he was to the lying ways of corporations. For me it was a new view of the media. For the first time they looked less like heroes than like posturing egomaniacs.

When it was all over, though, the news conference appeared to have gone about as well as any of us had dared to hope. The speech had worked, answering questions instead of giving rise to questions, and when it was finished none of the reporters had come up with questions that the Douglas people weren't ready to answer. I was delighted. I was also changed. In less than seventy-two hours I'd gone from being a stranger and an outsider at McDonnell Douglas to being almost a member of the family. And in the days that followed the news conference, as I compared what I now knew and what I'd witnessed with the often outlandish and consistently sensational things being printed and broadcast about the Paris crash and the DC-10, I changed further. I saw that it was possible for some businesspeople, at least, to conduct themselves quite admirably. I understood how it was that even the most honorable businesspeople so often regarded journalists as slime.

It was illuminating. It was also the first challenging and satisfying experience I'd had since going into public relations. The discovery that such an experience was possible in the agency business came as an immense relief.

Within a week after my return from California, McDonnell Douglas proposed and quickly signed a contract that made

Fleishman-Hillard its sole p.r. agency with an astonishing (to me) monthly retainer. And my boss no longer had to pretend that he was in charge of the work: the account was openly mine. And the work I did on the account continued to be more interesting, more satisfying, than anything else I was doing. Instead of being expected to come up with cheesy ways of getting the local media to take an interest in pointless little publicity stunts, I was now trying to get the facts about the DC-10 and the Paris crash known around the world while fending off wild blows from the heavyweight media. Instead of writing perky little releases about some new snack food or how much the St. Louis Snabbet Company had earned in the third quarter, I was, for the first time in my life, playing on an international stage.

I loved the scope of it, the seriousness. I loved working with the top people at Douglas Aircraft and at McDonnell Douglas headquarters. It's not possible to help people face the slings and arrows of an outraged press corps without finding out pretty quickly whether those people know what they're talking about and whether they're willing to talk straight. The people at Douglas Aircraft usually knew what they were talking about. When they didn't, they had the sense to keep silent.

Old Mac himself, the corporation's founder, was a near genius with a will of iron. Though he was in his mid-seventies and a few years before had handed the CEO title to his nephew, what he said was law. He was endlessly demanding, always questioning, and he expected the people who worked for him to give him answers that would hold up under pressure. The people who reported directly to him were, accordingly, an impressive and in many ways a surprising group. For example, Dick Davis, the communications vice president, was a man of a kind I never would have expected to find in the upper reaches of corporate p.r. Keenly intelligent, he was bookish and introspective, a native New Yorker who'd grown up during the Depression, become a *Newsweek* correspondent in Washington after the war, and spent the rest of his life worshiping the memories of FDR, Harry Truman, and the New Deal. Dick had the sad, baggy face of an ancient hound but wide interests and a robust sense of humor. It was easy to spend hours talking with him about politics and history and baseball. Dealing with people like these—especially since I could deal with them as a consultant, a bright young man from the outside world, an equal—transformed my perceptions of McDonnell Douglas.

Soon McDonnell Douglas was Fleishman-Hillard's biggest client. Before going to California I'd been in danger of becoming a kind of problem child around the office, a malcontent, a semipathetic former reporter who'd tried to cross over to the world of commerce and somehow had gotten stuck halfway between the two. All of a sudden I was a top producer, a bringer in, of big money. They made me a partner and a vice president. Nobody was more amazed by all this than I.

The next big lurch came one day when Dick Davis called and asked if I could be at his office that afternoon. Sandy McDonnell, president of McDonnell Douglas and Old Mac's nephew, wanted to see us. I remember being grateful that I'd worn my best suit to work that day. I assumed that Sandy and Dick were going to give me an assignment of some kind—a speech to write, probably.

What they had for me wasn't an assignment but the offer of a job. Sandy, a thin, long-limbed man of inextinguishable good nature, said they wanted to talk with me about the fact that Dick was sixty years old, hoped to retire in another five years, and didn't have a successor on his staff. That gave rise to a proposition: if I would leave the agency and go on the McDonnell Douglas payroll they would make me the number-two man in the communications department. And though no promises were possible, Sandy said, it was his hope that in five years they'd find me ready for Dick's job. Meanwhile, for starters, they could offer a 25 percent bump in salary plus an annual bonus plus the kind of pension plan that can't be found at an agency plus a parking spot inside the headquarters building plus plus plus plus plus.

I took a weekend to think it over and to talk it over with Pam, but the decision wasn't hard for either of us. What was there to decide, really? Here was the only client I'd ever really enjoyed, and now they were offering me a chance to link up with them permanently, with a nice jump in pay and all those other pluses and an inside shot at a *really* big job in another five years. In another five years I'd barely be forty. On the other side of the coin, I suspected that if I didn't accept Sandy's offer my chances of maintaining McDonnell Douglas as a high-retainer client were probably close to nil. The McDonnells, all of them, prided themselves on being skinflint Scotsmen. Before the Paris crash the corporation had never used a public relations agency. I felt certain that it wouldn't be long before they reverted to form. Then I'd be back where I'd started: forcing myself to do work I found worse than meaningless for clients I'd rather not have met.

Even at that point what I really wanted was simply to go back to the *Post-Dispatch*. The same old managing editor was still on duty, though, and I'd have walked barefoot to McDonnell Douglas on sidewalks covered with broken glass before asking for his help again. So when Monday arrived I called Dick Davis and told him he could tell Sandy that I'd decided to accept.

Dick rejoiced. Later he reported that Sandy too was rejoicing.

Everybody was delighted. I tried to persuade myself that I too was delighted. Was I at least a little uneasy about the fact that, a bare four years after escaping from the corporate world, I had allowed myself to be drawn back in?

You bet I was. Even at that point I knew down deep that my whole life—my whole so-called career—was headed in the wrong direction and starting to pick up speed.

But there seemed to be no way to turn around. I couldn't see what to do except to go with it and hope for the best.

49

ANYTHING FOR publicity. That should be our battle cry. At Aaron D. Cushman & Associates we will do almost anything to get almost any kind of publicity for Century 21.

USA Today is planning a story on the state of the housing market in cities across the country. Several of us spend days, spend a week or more, collecting information and feeding it to the reporter. Everything we do will be charged to Century 21 at rates upward of a hundred dollars per hour per staff member.

When the story ran it was a big one, prominently displayed and constructed largely out of what we provided. But Century 21 is mentioned only once, and not prominently. This is far from a coup. It's more a bitter disappointment, actually. One of my yuppie crew members, almost distraught, calls up the reporter and complains. Understandably. Without good clips—copies of newspaper stories trumpeting the importance of Century 21 in the real estate business—we have no way of justifying our bills.

As for the *size* of those bills . . . Oy. Aaron D. Cushman is staffed and structured on the assumption that it can pull at least thirty thousand dollars a month out of Century 21.

Obsessed with finding new ways to bill more hours (that's what our life here is focused on, billable hours), I think of weekly newspapers and how hungry they often are for stories with some kind of local angle. I think of how many weeklies there are in suburban and small-town America, and of how many press clippings (our stock in trade) we could generate by giving the editors of those weeklies something they would be willing to print.

I send a message to Century 21's regional managers around the country, asking if they'd be interested in a supply of ready-made real estate advice columns. We at Cushman would produce the columns, and they, the regional managers, could then send them out to the company's thousands of franchised offices. The owners and managers of those offices could then put their own names on the columns and offer them to their local weeklies without charge. Voilà: instant publicity for the local people. Far more importantly, lots of clips bearing the Century 21 name. Fame for them, fortune for us. If not fortune, survival.

The regional managers love the idea. So I get an armful of books about residential real estate from the library and start writing short sermons about how to sell a house fast, how to decide how much to ask for your house, how to make your office more appealing . . .

I show my first batch of columns to Tom Amberg, who loves them. Then I send them to Century 21's communications vice president, Monte Helm, for his okay. He hates them. He calls and tells me what shoddy work this is, what a sad excuse for a writer I am. Shaken, I ask him for more specific comments. He doesn't really have any. I promise to try to do better.

Monte Helm is the man who insisted on the replacement of my predecessor. Now he seems to be out for my skin, I know not why. Back at the office we decide that I will continue to write the columns—Tom assures me that he still thinks the ones I've produced are fine—but that from now on they will be sent to Helm as Tom's work. This ruse works; Helm is pacified. But I'm still in the doghouse with the only good client we have.

Helm, I'm convinced, has some kind of schoolboy crush on Amberg. Even if both of them are married and very straight and Helm himself is sixty years old and a grandfather. Anybody who gets between him and Amberg, I think, is going to be in trouble.

This is not only the most unpleasant working situation I've been in in years, it's also the most unstable. It can't last.

Ah, the life of a senior vice president.

50

If NOBODY WILL give you a job, *buy* yourself one. That's the idea behind franchising. You throw a hunk of money into somebody else's business idea, and what you get back (you hope) is a little business of your own and a dependable living wage.

I've started checking out Mail Boxes Etc. For an investment of about a hundred grand you can open a shop where people bring things to be packed and shipped. While you've got them on the premises you can sell them ballpoint pens, greeting cards, money orders, the use of your copying machine. It's one of the fastest-growing franchise operations in the country.

Pam hates the idea. I ask if she has a better one. Whenever the subject comes up, both of us get hot. The local Mail Boxes rep gives me a list of franchisees in Wisconsin and Illinois. I start using my Saturdays to drive from shop to shop and talk with the owners.

In downtown Evanston, one block from Northwestern University, I meet a woman whose shop is obviously doing well. But the location is exceptional: a big residential university, a high-income suburb, a booming business district. This woman bought her franchise early. All the locations this good were grabbed up years ago.

In Wheaton, a friendly, big-bellied man tells me that, yes, it definitely is possible to make a good living out of a Mail Boxes store.

Eventually. If you're willing to work hard and operate in the red for quite a while. "Of course if you're expecting to make thirty or forty thousand a year," he says with a smile, "that may be a very different matter."

Near Chicago's North Shore is a man who says he's doing very well indeed. As we talk, however, he mentions that he also has a patronage job with Cook County—a job that gives him a full-time salary with benefits for putting in three or four hours a week. Not exactly a useful example.

In a strip mall in a raw new suburb I come upon a Mail Boxes owned and operated by a thin, bald man who looks harried despite the emptiness of his establishment. When I tell him what I want he takes me behind the counter, offers me a chair, seats himself at his desk. In response to my questions he tells me how he was outplaced by the corporation where he'd been employed as an accountant, failed to find another job, and with great difficulty persuaded his wife that they should take their accumulated retirement money and buy him a job.

I tell him that if I buy a Mail Boxes franchise it absolutely *must* do well enough to support me after the first two years. I ask him if that sounds realistic.

The man bursts into tears, actually begins to sob. He pulls a handkerchief out of his pocket and starts mopping at his eyes.

"I'm sorry," he says. "I'm sorry. I'll be all right in a minute."

How very encouraging.

PART V

McDonnell Douglas

Up and Out

5I

WHAT HAPPENED to me on the payroll of McDonnell Douglas Corporation shouldn't have come as a surprise. It was actually predicted by one of my friends from the *Post-Dispatch,* a middle-aged copy editor from the Deep South who'd never gone to college but was among the best-read, best-informed, most perceptive people I'd ever met. He'd educated himself, he told me once, by reading the *Encyclopaedia Britannica* from beginning to end. He was one of the few people in the world of whom I would have believed such a thing. Pam happened to have a talk with him not long after I'd taken the McDonnell Douglas job, and when she told him the news he shook his head and said I was making a big mistake.

"Oh, I don't think so," Pam replied. "He's been consulting for them for over a year now. He seems to know exactly what he's getting into."

"Tell him this for me," my friend said. "Tell him the prison looks completely different when they lock the doors behind you."

I laughed when I heard that. It was ridiculous. Never in my life had I ever been given such a good look at a place before having to decide whether to work there.

But it turned out that my friend was right. Playing the role of the savvy consultant who drops in when something important needs doing and stays away when things are slow—that was one thing. Becoming a mere employee of one of the biggest, slowest-moving corporate bureaucracies in America, having to sit down at the same green metal desk early every morning and stay at it all day whether there was work to be done or not—that was something very different. It felt *exactly* like having the doors of a prison slam behind you. Everything went dark and dead. Gradually I found that though I still had contact with the big guys whose job it was to grapple with the big issues, such contact was less frequent and more oblique. When I had such contact now it was as a surbordinate, someone with a defined place in the hierarchy and therefore someone easily taken for granted. Though I still sometimes had challenging work to do, the periods when I did were increasingly few and brief. As time passed and the worst of our DC-10 problems subsided, such periods became even fewer and briefer. I was part of the machine now, one of the corporation's hundred thousand functionaries.

A woman who was my secretary for several years at McDonnell Douglas told me shortly before she retired that when she looked back on her years at the company she felt as if she'd spent them in "some kind of compound." She, like the friend who tried to warn me about prison doors, had it right. For tens of thousands of its employees, McDonnell Douglas was a gulag. They were generously compensated inmates (not many would have stayed without the good pay and the medical insurance and the pension plan and the rest) shuffling from one day to the next in a kind of low-grade depression governed by an immense body of obscure rules.

There were rules about everything, but most of them were invisible until you collided with them. I collided with them regularly, even when I decided to start using my lunch hours for jogging. I found a building with a shower in it, and on the first day of what I expected to be my new noontime routine I changed clothes and set off at a trot out the gate and down the road. Half an hour or so later, as I was returning, two uniformed members of the company's security force pulled up in a station wagon and waved me to a halt.

"*Man,* we've had a lot of calls about you!"

"Calls? About me? What kind of calls?"

"Calls from people reporting you. Maybe you don't realize you're breaking two company rules."

"Two rules?"

"You're running on company property. And you're wearing short pants on company property. Those are both against the rules." They put me in the backseat of the station wagon, drove me to my clothes, and told me not to do it again. I didn't do it again. As for the thought that I was working among people who would rush to call the authorities if they saw a jogger outside their office windows—that was almost too much to bear.

One day at lunchtime the cashier's office, which cashed checks for employees in a steady stream almost all day long, suddenly wouldn't accept one from me—a small one issued by the company to repay me for taking a visiting reporter to dinner. The woman on the other side of the window explained that it was against the rules for the McDonnell Douglas cashier's office to cash a check issued by McDonnell Douglas.

"Goddamn!" I exploded to a man who'd been waiting in line with me, a good-natured low-level administrator who'd been with the company for more than twenty years. "Where *are* all these goddamned rules? Are they written *down* somewhere?"

"Not that I know of," my companion said.

"Then how the hell do you find out what they are?"

"You break them. Then you find out."

As the problems created by the Paris crash continued to fade, the communications department in which I was now the number-two executive gradually sank into what was, I realized with foreboding, its accustomed torpor. Throughout the headquarters building, spirits and energy seemed chronically low. Nobody seemed to have much to do or to be particularly interested in whatever work came along. If I suggested something new, as I did with decreasing frequency, I was almost always told it wasn't possible. The reason usually turned out to be somebody's interpretation of something that Old Mac supposedly had said twenty-five years ago. It was Meredith Publishing Company all over again, this time with badges. Everybody at McDonnell Douglas had to wear a badge. The badges were of different colors to make it easy to tell the important people from the ones who didn't much matter and the ones who scarcely existed.

I'd made a clean escape from Meredith's only to fall into exactly the same thing all over again six years later. What was wrong with me?

Belatedly I came to understand that the company I was working for wasn't the McDonnell Douglas I had seen in California—a glamorous supplier of jet planes for airlines around the world—but the biggest defense contractor in America. Nine tenths of the things that my secretary dropped into my in-basket were about weapons systems and military appropriations and the intrigues of congressional subcommittees. All of us—the whole corporation, most definitely the division that built the DC jetliners and usually sold them at a loss—were supported by the Pentagon. By fighter planes and rockets and missiles. Everything around me, from the salaries of all these tens of thousands of people to the big cars in the headquarters garage and the vast wealth of the McDonnell family—had come from the American taxpayer.

Socialism for the rich? Welfare for the white and healthy and well-educated? Whatever it was, it didn't seem to trouble anybody. One day, at a boardroom meeting where some consultant from Washington was telling us how alleged abuses in military procurement were threatening to become a hot political issue, the man seated at my left looked over at me slyly. "Why the hell," he whispered with a smirk, "don't they go after the welfare cheats?" This was the one called Jimmy Mac, Old Mac's eldest son. He was the owner of just short of two million shares of McDonnell Douglas stock, each share worth about eighty dollars at the time. He was a vice president, but it was never clear to me just what he actually did.

Total dependence on Pentagon contracts distorted the environment in powerful ways. It made the senior people in the divisions that built the fighter planes and other military hardware—men I hadn't met while consulting on DC-10 problems—as arrogant and ingrown a fraternity as I'd ever encountered. Their products were making everybody in the company's upper reaches very rich very rapidly, and therefore they knew they were smart. The divisions they managed were based in St. Louis, where Old Mac himself made his start, and when they looked westward to Douglas Aircraft (which Old Mac had merely bought when the Douglas family fell on hard times) what they saw was the limitless folly of the commercial aircraft business, Hollywood Babylon, a bottomless sewer down which a river of profits (including a great deal of money that could have gone into bigger bonuses) was being poured. These people from the military side of the company were almost unanimously infected with the paranoia that had been so noticeable and seemed so laughable when I first visited the company. I wasn't laughing now. These were people who seemed to believe that anyone who wasn't with them was against them. Quite often they seemed to believe that anyone who wasn't *them* was against them.

The senior people on the commercial side, the Douglas people I'd first met when I was sent to California, feared and resented their counterparts on the military side. They blamed the military side—and corporate headquarters as well—for not being bold enough or imaginative enough to invest the millions needed to make the company an effective competitor in the international commercial aircraft business. Without the killjoys in St. Louis, the commercial people believed, Douglas Aircraft could be as strong and as profitable as Boeing.

McDonnell Douglas was a house divided. It was Athens versus Sparta, with the Athenians in California and the Spartans in St. Louis. The Spartans were completely dominant. I myself have always been partial to Athenians.

For nearly two years I sat at my desk and tried to tell myself how lucky I was. I had the semi-exalted title of corporate director of external relations, and my badge was silver on top and gold on the bottom, the second-best kind of badge you could get. I had this swell salary and nearly as much job security as if I were working for the government . . .

And I hated it. With every month that went by I was a little more depressed and a little more resentful, and gradually I started behaving as depressed as I felt and showing my resentment. I could tell that my former client and now boss, Dick Davis, saw what was happening to me and was concerned. It was equally obvious that he didn't know what to do. I didn't know what to do either. We never talked about it; we weren't talking much about anything anymore; I was avoiding him. I could see what was coming. I would decay at my desk, and when the time finally arrived for Dick to retire everybody would agree that giving his job to this poor strange guy Meyer was simply out of the question. Somebody else would be brought in as the new vice president—maybe an outsider, maybe some bright young guy from one of the divisions—and when that happened my depression and resentment would become terminal. Eventually Dick's successor would either throw me out or move me into some remote part of the bureaucracy where I would be allowed to accumulate enough points for retirement. There were a good many such pieces of human wreckage in the deepest recesses of McDonnell Douglas.

I felt like a man in a small and leaky raft, drifting slowly slowly slowly toward some immense waterfall but finding it impossible to act. I was paralyzed. A year at McDonnell Douglas slowly became two and then three, and occasionally I would have a spasm of energy and write to some newspaper to ask about work, but nothing ever came of it. Once, to my astonishment, I got a call from Ben Bradlee, the executive editor of *The Washington Post.* On the phone he was as profane as his reputation, and profanely he told me he'd read my clips and was impressed. "Don't get fucking excited, though," he said. "I'm not gonna offer you a fucking job. I fucking don't have a job to offer you." The managing editor of the *Minneapolis Tribune* did offer me a job, but the salary he offered was pitiful. Even so, sensing how miserable I was in spite of my reluctance to talk much about it (I found it embarrassing), Pam did some checking to see if she could find work in the Twin Cities. She had no luck. We had three kids in private schools now, and one of them was having recurrent major surgery for the repair of a birth defect. Moving five hundred miles north on one inadequate salary would have been madness.

And what reason was there to expect that my job woes would be solved if we went to Minneapolis or some other new place? It seemed more and more probable that the root of the problem was not in these jobs but in me. That I would be miserable wherever I went and therefore in serious danger of failing spectacularly whatever I did. This was not a pleasant line of thought.

As Ben Bradlee probably would have put it, I was one fucking fucked fucker. With nobody to blame but myself.

And then, amazingly, another DC-10 fell out of the sky one afternoon and again my life changed completely. The details were a little different this time: Chicago instead of Paris, an engine falling off instead of a door, two hundred and seventy-five people killed instead of three hundred and forty-six, American Airlines instead of Turkish Airlines. But it was exactly the same kind of crisis—more calls than we could return from impatient, indignant journalists, reports from around the world that people were again afraid of DC-10s—and this time the crisis climaxed in a decision by the Federal Aviation Administration to ground every DC-10 in America. Other countries followed. In those days a new DC-10 cost roughly thirty million dollars, and around the world something over two hundred DC-10s were in service. And suddenly none of them was allowed to carry passengers. Suddenly all those machines on which airlines had spent billions of dollars had no value at all.

It was an immense tragedy—all those charred corpses just for starters—and it brightened my life. As after Paris, the amount of work that urgently needed doing was practically unlimited. Throwing myself into that work was like waking up from an ugly, migrainy kind of trance. For my boss, by contrast, it appeared to be one crisis too many. Now it was Dick's turn to seem demoralized. He didn't resist as I took over more and more of the work. His relief was obvious, in fact. He seemed exhausted, his attention focused on retirement. So I took over much of the work flow, he receded into a kind of grandfatherly oversight role, and we became friends again. At the end of long, eventful days I'd brief him on what had been happening and what I was doing, and we'd put our feet up on his coffee table and talk awhile about General Marshall or Babe Ruth or other selections from the huge array of subjects that Dick found interesting and knew a lot about. Then he'd pack up his briefcase and head for home, and I'd get back to work.

Grant and Sherman and Stonewall Jackson all were strange, deficient men who were failures in peacetime but made themselves indispensable when a hard, bad war came. I find it easy to identify with them. The Chicago DC-10 disaster lifted me out of a slide to certain failure and created a situation, an emergency, in which for some reason I found it easy to outshine all the people who outshone me when things were calm. Without the Chicago disaster I would have had no future—certainly none at McDonnell Douglas.

During the years when we were digging out of that disaster—and the process did take years—Old Mac suddenly became very ill and soon died. His nephew Sandy became CEO in fact as well as in title. This simply made my continued transformation more certain than ever, because Sandy for some reason had always been my champion on the top floor. When Dick Davis retired on schedule there seemed to be little question about who was going to replace him. And I had no doubts about whether I was capable of replacing him. In many respects I'd replaced him, taken over for him, already. All I had to do was move into the big corner office with the teak furniture and the private bathroom and pretty much go on with what I'd been doing.

That's how it happened. How, at forty, I arrived.

Did I then learn to love McDonnell Douglas? Not really. Certainly not without reservations. It was still a vast and rigid bureaucracy, bound in red tape and hostile not only to change but often, it seemed, to creativity in any form. Too many of the people inside it still looked miserably unhappy to me. Many of the people at its highest levels still seemed invincibly arrogant, and the leaders of its various divisions still hated one another bitterly.

But these sorts of things don't weigh you down so heavily when you're at the top of the pyramid. When you have a splendid office, and when you're the one who decides what work is going to get done and who's going to do it, it's hard to feel oppressed. When you have a cheerful, supportive boss who responds positively every time you tell him which changes you've decided to make next, it's hard to curse your fate. When you can get on a plane and go to either coast or to Europe or Asia not only whenever you need to but almost whenever you want, life can start to taste pretty sweet. I had all these things now. And though my supplies of common sense are obviously limited, they were more than adequate to make me see that this time I really *was* a lucky S.O.B.

I was free, and I tried to use my freedom to make my own department less hidebound, less bureaucratic, more lively and human. One by one I got the worst of the department's bureaucrats moved to other areas. I found improbable replacements for some of them: a woman trained as a painter to run the employee paper, a young poet to become a trainee in media relations, the head of *Business Week*'s London bureau to focus on international p.r. We started shutting down operations that didn't seem to have much real purpose and replacing them with new things—new programs, new publications, experiments that were successful more often than not. I judged the success of these changes in part according to whether my recruits found the environment tolerable and were able to stay with us. Most of them not only stayed but seemed happy to do so. Together we dreamed up more experiments. For me, going to work started to be more fun than it ever had been.

All my life I've been hearing people say that to be a good leader you first have to be a good follower. Teachers say this, and coaches and Scout leaders, and low-level foremen and supervisors. I think it's pure baloney. I think they say it to try to get us to behave ourselves so that their lives will be easier. I hated being a mid-level functionary at McDonnell Douglas. I did a very bad job as a mid-level functionary. If I'd had to remain a functionary I'd have been destroyed one way or another, by slow disintegration if not in an explosion. But as soon as I escaped upward I became not just happy—as happy as a man of my peculiarities is likely ever to be in such an environment—but also productive.

There were still shadows, and some of them had been growing steadily darker ever since the death of Old Mac. The fault lines within the corporation were getting deeper and more dangerous, with lethal political struggles going on constantly just beyond Sandy McDonnell's range of vision. I was spared most of the effects of this by the fact that I reported directly to Sandy, who always made it plain to everybody that I had his confidence and support. We had an implicit deal: I did what I thought was right, I kept him informed, and he shielded me from the politics. When some of the most powerful of the Spartans told me they wanted to run national ads in support of higher defense spending (these were the early Reagan years, mind you, when defense spending was already spiraling crazily upward) I said no. When they tried to insist, I said the idea was preposterous and if tried would be self-defeating. They said they were going to appeal to Sandy. I told them that was their right, but it wouldn't do them any good. That was the end of it.

The Spartans were learning to hate me, but that was their problem. Or so I thought.

These disputes could get ugly. Defense spending and defense profits were mounting year after year thanks to Reagan and Caspar Weinberger, and at the same time the airliner business was falling into a deep and dangerous slump. The power of the Spartans was visibly greater every year, and the world in which they made their money, the world of Pentagon contracts, was growing constantly more political. The more powerful the Spartans became, the more the money poured in, the more you could see their attention shifting from design and manufacturing—the product quality that Old Mac had made the McDonnell Douglas hallmark—to games of a kind that could only be played in Washington. The Spartans started hiring more and more freshly retired senior military officers, not because such people had technical or business skills that anyone could possibly find useful but in the expectation that such people could open doors to the offices of the not-yet-retired people who handed out the contracts. Traditionally, under Mr. Mac, McDonnell Douglas had been better than most defense companies at staying away from this sort of game. But the defense business was changing rapidly and for the worse, and all the big aerospace companies were changing with it. The industry was starting to become almost as decadent as the shrillest critics of the Military Industrial Complex had always assumed, wrongly, that it actually must be.

The Spartans were even starting to say that if we hired the right kinds of p.r. people—freshly retired public affairs officers from the military service, preferably—we could not only open a few more doors in Washington but probably get the news media to start doing our bidding at last. This really was ridiculous, and again I said no. The Spartans were increasingly unhappy with me, but it didn't seem to matter.

The poor Athenians, meanwhile, were being shoved more and more to the margins. Their future seemed increasingly in doubt.

In the midst of all this, the company was being prodded into a sort of examination of conscience. Sandy McDonnell had carried with him into the chairmanship a gnawing fascination with moral questions and a zealous desire to bring "cultural change" to the corporation. He introduced programs in ethical decision-making, delivered speeches about employee empowerment, and in other ways revealed a surprising degree of awareness—surprising to some of us, offensive or pathetic to others—of the company's limitations. He displayed an almost passionate desire to change things for the better.

What he didn't bring to the chairmanship, unfortunately, was even a trace of his uncle's obsessive attention to detail. Mr. Mac had kept up with everyone, pried into everything. As a result, he was able to make sure that his people knew their work and were doing it. Sandy, by contrast, was susceptible to being impressed by an executive's ability to display (or to feign) enthusiasm for his ideas of cultural change. He paid too little attention to what that same executive might actually be doing, how he might be behaving, when the big boss wasn't around.

Sandy evolved into a kind of preacher in a pulpit high above the McDonnell Douglas congregation. His eyes lifted to the heavens, he could talk endlessly about organizational self-renewal and ethics and ignore almost everything else. Beneath him in the pews Sandy's disciples shouted Amen and smiled broadly whenever he gazed down upon them. When he raised his eyes again they would pull out their knives and go back to dismembering one another. The old iron discipline of McDonnell Douglas dissolved into behind-the-scenes bloodshed and chaos. Cost and production problems of a kind rarely before seen at the corporation began to pop up, sporadically at first and then with disturbing frequency. The Spartans found themselves free—so long as they remembered to shout Hallelujah at the right moments—to use their knives not just on the Athenians but, increasingly, on one another. Meanwhile, billions of dollars poured into the coffers not just of McDonnell Douglas but of every defense contractor in the country, and company after company set new records every year for sales and profits. Success appeared to be guaranteed, so nobody worried much about it.

I wasn't worried. Not about myself, certainly. Because I had such a big job with such a big and prosperous company, and because I was barely into my mid-forties, headhunters lusted for me in those days. They called regularly. Usually I paid no attention.

I did look into a few things, though. I made several visits to Abbott Laboratories in Chicago. On the last of these visits the Abbott people asked me to bring Pam along, and they arranged for us to look at houses in Chicago's posh Gold Coast suburbs. Finally they made me an offer that would have put my salary into an entirely new category and festooned me with stock options. I agonized over that one for a while, and then I turned it down.

So McDonnell Douglas wasn't perfect? Welcome to the real world. Life at McDonnell Douglas was morally ambiguous? Tell me what isn't. McDonnell Douglas, I decided, was good enough. It allowed Pam and me to have, away from work, exactly the life we wanted. It was a good life for both of us, for the kids, for my parents. And that was more than good enough. That was *good*.

Abbott Laboratories was a watershed. After that I stopped thinking about other jobs, other careers, escapes to something that somehow might be closer to perfection. From that point all I wanted was more of the same: to stay in my job and try to make the best of it, to get my kids raised and launched, to prepare for a retirement that if things continued to go so well might possibly come early. I was ready to see how good I could get at simply enjoying life.

If it wasn't the career I'd dreamed of, big deal. My career dreams had always been too fuzzy to be of any real use.

Was I being realistic? Why not? Every time I had a performance review, Sandy ladled praise on me. During one of the last of these reviews I told him about my disagreements with the Spartans, with the chief of the Spartans in particular. He told me not to worry. The chief of the Spartans didn't get along with anybody, he said.

The work we were doing in the communications department was winning national awards. When I'd been in the corner office for five years, the *Washington Journalism Review* conducted a survey of reporters and editors across the country to find out which corporate p.r. operations they regarded as the best and which they thought were the worst. McDonnell Douglas was listed among the best.

In my seventh year *The Wall Street Journal* did a survey that measured reader opinion of the eighteen biggest aerospace companies in the country. In every category, McDonnell Douglas was rated second or third, with Boeing always in first place. Considering that we were constantly in trouble—accused of stealing from the government, of building airliners that weren't safe, of producing missiles that couldn't have hit Canada if they were launched from Maine—I was relieved and a little surprised to see us doing so well. Considering that we were consistently near the bottom of the aerospace industry in terms of financial performance (our profits, though immense in raw dollar terms, were anemic as a percentage of our far more immense sales), the high rating we got as an investment bordered on the miraculous. Where communications was concerned, McDonnell Douglas seemed to be doing miraculously well.

In 1988 Sandy McDonnell retired and was succeeded as chairman and CEO by his cousin John, Old Mac's second son. I'd known John McDonnell since joining the company, had worked with him often, and thought—assumed, I should say in retrospect—that he had a reasonably good opinion of me. I thought well of him, certainly. I knew him to be intelligent, unassuming, and almost neurotically hardworking.

But then a reorganization was announced and I wasn't reporting to the CEO anymore. From now on I'd be reporting to a man who was as improbable a senior aerospace executive as I, a senior vice president who was a graduate of Princeton Theological Seminary, had met Sandy McDonnell while doing community development work, and had been brought into the company to work with Sandy on cultural change. Once inside he proved to be a political genius. He rocketed up through the organization past all the thousands of engineers and business school graduates, becoming in the process the most loathed individual in the entire corporation. I wasn't happy about having to report to him, but I was prepared to make the best of it, especially after I was assured that my disconnection from the CEO's office hadn't happened because anyone was unhappy with me or my performance. "Reporting to," I reasoned, could turn out to mean "under the protection of." Being under the protection of the best politician around might be almost as acceptable as being out of the company's politics completely.

Little by little, though, things kept changing. From my first arrival as a consultant to McDonnell Douglas I'd written every speech given by Mr. Mac and Sandy. But after becoming chairman John McDonnell hired an executive assistant—a young engineer with no experience in writing and no visible aptitude for it—and suddenly the assistant was expected to function as his speechwriter.

I found I wasn't being invited to as many meetings as in the past. And I was hearing more and more complaints from the Spartans: Why the hell was General Dynamics getting all this good press? Why the hell wasn't I able to do something about the *L.A. Times* (or *The Washington Post*, or *Die Welt*, or the *Yomiuri Shimbun*)?

The first big crisis of John's regime erupted early one Monday when a squad of United States marshals arrived at the fighter airplane plant and started seizing company files. The Justice Department in Washington told the media that this was being done because of allegations that McDonnell Douglas had been bribing Defense Department officials. The files were being impounded, the government told the world, to keep the company from burning them. It was a national scandal. A reporter sent to St. Louis by *The New York Times* took a room at a hotel near our headquarters and called to say she wanted to interview John McDonnell.

We had a meeting to decide what to do. John himself presided. Also present was my new boss the theologian, along with the company's chief legal counsel, two or three very senior Spartans, and a retired Air Force colonel who until recently had been Caspar Weinberger's press deputy and was now employed in the McDonnell Douglas Washington office as one of the corporation's expanding corps of door openers.

It didn't take long for me to see—by now I knew most of these people well enough to gauge such things quickly—that neither John nor the Spartans seriously feared that the government's accusations might be true. I was at least a little sorry to see this, having realized that a purge in Sparta might eliminate the most dangerous of my enemies. But instead of being defensive, John and the Spartans were indignant. I could tell they weren't pretending. Their assumption was that somebody in Washington— some rival contractor perhaps, or somebody on somebody's staff— had seen a chance to screw McDonnell Douglas and grabbed it.

The first question needing an answer was whether John should talk with the *Times* reporter. John turned to the lawyer and asked for his opinion. The lawyer said no, don't. This was predictable and not particularly significant: corporate lawyers are paid to say don't, and they never shirk their duty.

John turned to the colonel, who also said don't do it.

I was hoping that John would turn to me next. When he didn't, I spoke up anyway.

"I really think you ought to talk with her," I said. "Tell her that everything you know at this point convinces you there's not a shred of truth to this thing. But tell her also that you're going to look into the matter personally, and that your investigation is going to be more thorough than the government's. Tell her that if you find any evidence that anybody has done anything wrong you'll fix it so quickly and so completely that there won't be anything left for the government to do."

There was no response, so I plunged back in. "If you don't talk, everybody's going to assume we're guilty. The *Times* will clobber us, and every paper in the country will follow the *Times*. If you don't talk, even a lot of our own employees are going to wonder if we're guilty."

More silence.

Come on, John, I was thinking. Do it. You'll never regret it. You'll show the whole world, you'll show every man and woman in the company, that there's not a smarter or tougher CEO in the business. Or a more honest one.

Do it, John.

John looked at me without speaking and without expression for what seemed a long time.

Was I on the verge of being saved by yet another timely disaster?

Not this time. He turned away from me and looked again at the colonel.

Again the colonel shook his head: Don't do it.

John didn't do it. McDonnell Douglas and its CEO granted no interviews and issued no statements. Every day for a week and a half we took a shellacking not just in the *Times* but in every media outlet in the country. This happened despite the fact that the company was not actually guilty. Its innocence was established long afterward—long after the furor subsided, long after the damage had been done.

And was I vindicated by how things turned out? Not in the eyes of anyone at McDonnell Douglas. That meeting turned out to be the last time anyone at McDonnell Douglas ever allowed me to offer an opinion about anything.

On the sixth of June 1988, D day, I went to the theologian's office for our regular Monday morning meeting.

"God," he said, twisting in agony in his chair. "God, this is going to be hard!"

52

IMAGINE THAT somebody tries to kill you and makes a botch of it, so that after a horrifying struggle you find yourself bleeding from stab wounds and gunshot wounds, maimed but somehow still alive. That was what my firing at McDonnell Douglas was like. I expect I'll never know why they made such a mess of it.

The theologian, on the morning when he did the dirty deed, told me I was out "because we want new leadership in communications." Stunned as I've rarely been stunned in my life, almost overwhelmed by the thought of what this was going to mean for my family, I managed to ask him *why*. He didn't give me an answer. Nor did he answer when I asked *what* new leadership was wanted—who was going to take my place.

I asked if it was going to be the colonel, Caspar Weinberger's old press secretary. The colonel had been riding high since coming onto the McDonnell Douglas payroll two years before, flaunting his Pentagon and Republican connections. The Spartans thought he was their kind of guy. He was a tall, bald, pear-shaped, chinless man, soft and mottled with purple like the flesh of a snail. His personality mixed arrogance and unctuousness; he was a lot like what Uriah Heep would have been in his middle age. Many of the journalists who mattered to us had dealt with him in his Pentagon days. I believe they found him nearly as repulsive as I did.

"No," the theologian said. "It won't be him. I'm not comfortable with him."

He said the company would continue to pay me for up to six months, if necessary, while I looked for a new job. That sounded like a long time. I'd never been out of work, though. I had no idea how long finding work should be expected to take. My mouth went so dry I didn't think I could talk.

He said I should come back and see him the next morning, we would settle the details then. That, in retrospect, is the first really odd thing: that he didn't finish the job then and there, once and for all. That he didn't make a clean kill. Anybody who knows anything about firing people knows that you *never* let it drag out.

He led me out of his office and into a nearby conference room, where an executive-looking man I'd never seen before was waiting for me with a lugubrious smile. My first outplacement geek. He introduced himself, gave me his card, said he understood how difficult all this was but that he and his firm were going to be giving me a lot of help with my "transition." And yes, he did say that this might turn out to be the best thing that ever happened to me. My mouth had some moisture now, but I saw no point in trying to talk when I was feeling so angry and terrified. Finally I said that I just didn't feel ready to talk. He said he understood. He said I should go home for the rest of the week and we could get started the following Monday.

Back in my office I closed the door and sat alone for a long time, my mind in turmoil. My phone rang. It was McDonnell Douglas's chief financial officer, an older man who'd become a friend and a kind of mentor over the years. He asked if he could see me. Come on down, I said.

He already knew what had happened. I said I was finding it hard to believe. Thinking again about what this was going to mean for Pam and the kids, I started to say that I thought the whole thing was unbelievably unfair but choked up before I was half finished. The CFO was a tough-minded man. He said he thought I needed to accept the fact that there are no rules of fairness where the employment of senior executives is concerned. That the best thing was to accept this and move on.

"But there is one thing I want you to think about," he said. "I know they're offering you a separation package. What I'm not sure *you* know is that that package may be negotiable. I can't guarantee anything, and you have to be responsible for what you decide to do and how it turns out. But if I were you I wouldn't assume that what they've offered you is necessarily their final word."

I will go to my grave thinking that that visit was one of the kindest things anyone has ever done for me. But it added to the oddness of the situation. One of the highest executives at McDonnell Douglas was firing me, and was laying down terms. At almost the same moment an equally high executive was advising me not to be in a big hurry to accept those terms. I didn't know what to make of it. What I did know, on the basis of a great deal of experience, was that I could trust the CFO completely and shouldn't trust the theologian at all.

I drove downtown and called on a lawyer I knew socially, a specialist in employment discrimination. Walking from the garage to his office was a strange experience. All around me on the street were other men in suits and ties, men just like me, but now I felt myself to be a creature apart, marked, no longer a member in good standing of the old familiar world. It was as if I had eaten the fruit of the tree of the knowledge of good and evil, and would be forever different, forever cut off, as a result.

I told the lawyer what had just happened to me, asked him if I had any rights under the law. His answer surprised and disappointed me, and started me worrying about the soundness of the CFO's advice. At my level on the corporate ladder, he said, rights are small and few. He advised me to accept what McDonnell Douglas was offering and be thankful for it.

The hardest part came at the end of the day: breaking the news to Pam. Waiting to do it gave me an insight I'd never before had into the stories about men who lose their jobs and don't tell their wives, who get up every morning and put on their ties and pretend to go off to work. Now I understood. And I couldn't think of any way to do it except to just go ahead and do it—get it behind us.

Pam got home from work before I did. When I walked into the bedroom she was pulling off her stockings.

"I got fired today," I said.

"What?"

"They fired me. The bastards fired me."

"You shouldn't joke about a thing like that."

"I only wish I were joking." I crashed onto the bed and wrapped my arms around my head.

"Ho-ly shit," she said.

We spent the rest of the week absorbing the shock and trying to decide what to do next. I was focused on next Monday's meeting with the theologian.

After a lot of talk and a lot of worry I decided to disregard the lawyer's advice and say that six months' pay wasn't enough, that I was entitled to more and needed more. I thought it improbable that he'd agree, but I thought it equally improbable that he'd retaliate by withdrawing the original terms.

I was trying to think of some way to throw the theologian off balance, to loosen his control over the situation, when a peculiar idea came to mind. The more I thought about it, the more I liked it. I would take Pam to the meeting! She was a bright, strong, articulate, good-looking woman. There was a good chance that if she showed up the theologian would be flummoxed. When I told her what I was thinking her eyes got big. Then she smiled.

"Sure," she said. "Why not. He won't know *what's* going on!"

When Pam and I both walked into his office, the theologian was as surprised as I'd hoped he would be. "She has as much at stake in this as I do," I said by way of explanation. "I want her to hear it for herself." Without answering he got up and left the room. When he returned less than a minute later he had one of the company lawyers with him, tablet and pencil in hand. The lawyer had to have been waiting nearby.

I told them their offer was unacceptable. I said it was an inappropriate offer for a company officer who had been on the payroll for twelve years. I recited some words I'd rehearsed about how I had been recruited into the company from a good and secure position—comparing a partnership at Fleishman-Hillard, absurdly enough, with a tenured professorship. I talked about all the good offers I'd turned down since coming aboard, how good all my performance reviews had been. I laid out on the table various kinds of evidence of how well my department had been performing: magazine articles, opinion surveys, the like. I told them of how, since getting the ax, I had consulted a lawyer who had expertise in the employment field. Less truthfully, I suggested that "we" were prepared to seek legal remedies if the company wouldn't be reasonable. I tried to be firm and confident as I said these things. Pam managed to slip in some good stuff about the many people the two of us knew in the business media, not quite threatening but clearly insinuating that this could become a very interesting story.

All of it was a bluff, of course. If the theologian had responded by telling me that my choices were between his original offer and nothing, I would have surrendered on the spot. If he had ordered me out of the building, I probably would have begged his forgiveness. As for the idea that the media would take more than a small and fleeting interest in my dismissal, it was far-fetched to say the least. The theologian, however, wasn't likely to know that.

When we were finished—and again very oddly, it seems to me— the theologian said he wasn't prepared to respond. He needed more time, he said. He asked us to come back on Wednesday.

I spent Tuesday at the outplacement office, being shown around and given a general introduction to how the process worked. That was the day when I met other people from McDonnell Douglas whom I hadn't even known had been fired. Later, the visit proved to have been highly useful. I learned things I'd never known about headhunter directories, job-hunting guides, the basics of executive searches. These things made a big difference when I was looking for work on my own.

At home that night, Pam and I speculated about what was likely to happen next. We were, we agreed, totally at the company's mercy, totally without leverage.

The next morning, when we sat down in the theologian's office for yet another session, he lowered his head and glared at me through his eyebrows for what seemed a long time. He appeared to be in a state of barely contained rage, ready to leap across the table and tear my ears from my head. Not feeling threatened (the theologian was as pudgy as the colonel) but also not knowing what to do, I just sat there and looked back at him mildly. I thought of asking him if he was having a bad morning but decided not to. Finally he straightened up in his chair and with a tiny shake of his shoulders became something close to a normal person again. I assumed—still assume—that he'd decided to try to scare me and see how I'd react.

He said he'd given a great deal of thought to the things Pam and I had said on Monday. He said he found merit in some of those things. As a result, he had decided that I wasn't going to be fired after all.

What??

. . . But instead would be retained in my job except that from now on I would be reporting to the colonel . . .

Oh, Christ!!

. . . And everybody was sure that the whole thing was going to work out beautifully for all of us in the end. Meanwhile I could return to my office and my work.

Freshly stunned, totally unprepared for this, I walked Pam out to her car. I didn't understand any part of what had just happened. I don't understand it any better today. My guess is that the theologian had somehow failed to secure his flanks politically before moving on me, had blundered in not finishing the job and was left in an exposed position when I didn't surrender. His change, I'm sure, was less a reconsideration than an involuntary tactical retreat.

But *why* did he think it necessary to retreat? What was going on backstage? I'd love to know, but I don't think I ever will.

"Listen," I told Pam in McDonnell Douglas's vast headquarters parking lot, "we dodged a bullet today for some reason, but the bullet is coming back. I don't have any idea what's going on or why this happened, but there's no way that bastard is going to let this work out. We have to get out of here."

"Ohhh," said she, "you bet your ass."

53

THE COLONEL TOOK over my office, my secretary, and my work. I was left with my title, my salary, and nothing to do. It was Meredith Publishing yet again, with the spice of daily humiliation thrown in for good measure.

McDonnell Douglas could be uncharacteristically creative when its goal was to make life at work unbearable. I was put in a glass-walled office down a busy corridor from the colonel's office. Every day—I can't speak of workdays, because I no longer had any work—became an ordeal. Hour after hour I'd sit at my desk watching people pass back and forth outside my cage. When the people passing were friends or former members of my staff they'd give me little smiles and waves and look as uncomfortable as I felt. It was excruciating.

My new boss, the colonel, ignored my existence. Sometimes he would walk past the glass wall of my cell, and sometimes he'd be carrying a suit bag, heading off on trips that I'd have been taking if he hadn't been given my job. Sometimes important people passed by on their way to see him. These people never looked my way. In better days they'd have been on their way to see me. Now they studiously avoided looking my way. The colonel began to hire other colonels, former cronies from the Pentagon, not firing the old staff but putting them in limbo with me. The place was becoming a kind of junta, with platoons of retired military people presiding over a grotesquely swollen, grotesquely demoralized staff.

Taking action on my agreement with Pam—"We have to get out of here!"—I bought a stack of guidebooks on executive job-shopping. I wrote off for copies of the things I'd discovered during my day in outplacement—a directory with the name and address of every headhunter in the country, for example. And with the help of my former secretary (I didn't have one anymore), I got the hang of all the word-processing equipment in the department.

At night and on Saturdays I would slip back into the office, and like a mad scientist I would bring all the machinery in the communications department to life spitting out stacks of résumés and fat bundles of computer-customized letters addressed to headhunters by the score.

And I got my first sour taste of using the telephone as a spade for digging up job leads. I called every friend I could think, then every near-friend, and then mere acquaintances to tell them I was seriously in need of—no, that I'd decided to examine my options while figuring out if I really wanted to stay at McDonnell Douglas for the rest of my working life. I asked them to let me know if they heard of any interesting vacancies, no matter where. I'd never approached any of these people for this purpose before, and this was before the time when lots of people like me were in trouble and working the phones, so I got pretty good results. Turning up leads turned out to be not that hard.

Why was I looking everywhere in the country? Why, if our family life in St. Louis was so important, didn't I focus on finding a job at home?

I did, at first. But I soon learned that if you're in a specialty like p.r., and if you've had the top job in that specialty with a company as big as McDonnell Douglas, there are at most a few hundred jobs in the whole country for which you won't be considered grossly overqualified.

I learned also, by a process no more sophisticated than counting on my fingers, that among those two or three hundred possible jobs no more than half a dozen were within a hundred miles of home. And it didn't take much snooping to establish that in the summer of 1988 not one of those five or six local jobs was occupied by somebody even possibly inclined to move on.

I also learned something brutally ironic: that in the kind of world that the job seekers' guidebooks describe—and describe all too accurately, I think—home can be the worst place in the world to look for work. The important fiction that I was still firmly attached to McDonnell Douglas, that I was therefore a prize to be wooed and won, could be expected to work in the early stages at least in Chicago and New York and Atlanta. Those were places where nobody who mattered knew me or knew McDonnell Douglas. But closer to home any captain of industry who started making inquiries about me would quickly learn, over the grapevine if not by running into some member of the McDonnell family or one of their retainers at the country club or symphony hall, that I was now a discard. Once that became known, all the guidebooks agreed, my employability quotient would start a rapid slide toward zero.

The process of getting a new job was going to be a form of theater. I was going to have to be an illusionist. At close range the illusion couldn't be made to work. If I wanted to remain an "executive"—and what else was I going to do?—we were going to have to make a run for it.

It was theater. Looked at another way, it was also very like the kind of fishing I'd done with a cane pole and a bobber when I was a boy. There was no way of predicting which of all the head-hunters in the country might get an assignment involving a job that might make sense for me. There was no way of knowing which of my friends and near-friends and acquaintances might be called by a headhunter looking for candidates. Every résumé I put in the mail, every call I made, was another line in the water, another bobber on the surface of a vast pond. A job search was a matter of putting as many lines in the water as possible—hundreds and hundreds of lines. Once the surface of the pond was crowded with bobbers, it became a matter of watching for nibbles.

Getting nibbles turned out to be not terribly difficult that first time around. The spending binge first ignited by Ronald Reagan's deficits hadn't quite run out of steam, so the economy was still lively. Corporations were still hiring. Probably more importantly, I was still a mere lad of forty-seven—still a safe distance from the lethal half-century mark.

Did I consider myself lucky to be getting nibbles? Not really—not then. I took my nibbles almost for granted. This was a time, remember, when my string was still unbroken: I'd been working for thirty-five years, and in all that time I'd never had a job interview that hadn't led to an offer. It seemed reasonable to expect that I might soon be looking at more dancing bobbers than any one angler could possibly hope to handle.

And that's more or less the way things worked out. Nights and weekends I kept cranking up the laser printers and churning out more and more résumés for the morning mail. My old secretary, proving herself a real friend, handled a lot of the typing (the colonel had very little for her to do). And our labors brought results. It took only a few weeks for me to get into hot contention for a juicy job with Continental Bank in Chicago. And though I eventually came in second in that race, by the time the winner beat me to the finish line I didn't much care. I was already interviewing at two other places: J. I. Case and The Travelers Insurance Company of Hartford, Connecticut.

The job at The Travelers looked good at first. The company was huge and venerable, one of the giants of the American insurance industry. The sums it controlled were unimaginably huge—scores of billions of dollars. Its offices reflected its wealth. So did its ways of doing business. When I flew to Hartford for interviews I was met by a limousine and driver. On a few of these trips I had to go through New York, and when that happened a richly appointed company helicopter would pick me up at the south end of Manhattan and whisk me north to Connecticut. After my first few visits The Travelers sent a consulting psychologist to St. Louis to meet and evaluate me. Even more than McDonnell Douglas, this was big business. *Big* business.

But the charms of The Travelers tended to fade under close scrutiny. On my first few trips to Hartford I was watching expectantly for signs of New England charm, but gradually it became clear that little of the kind was to be found in that particular neck of the woods. The company itself appeared to combine the stolidity traditionally associated with insurance offices with the stomach-churning insecurity of organizations in trouble.

The Travelers, I found when I started looking into it, was in a kind of trouble rarely, until recently, seen among the grand old monoliths of the insurance industry. Its leaders had made some big and outlandishly foolish investments—had been swindled, actually—and its financial position was badly eroded as a result. And The Travelers was still managed by the same people who had been managing it when it got into trouble. As I made the interview rounds and began to meet those people I saw that they were an edgy, frayed-nerves bunch. I saw too, now that McDonnell Douglas had attuned me to some of the subtleties of bureaucratic architecture, that the top layers of management at The Travelers were arranged in dangerously Byzantine ways.

The job for which I was competing—vice president of public relations—reported to a lawyer named Peter LiBasse, who held the title of senior vice president. LiBasse, in turn, reported to an executive vice president, who reported to the chairman and CEO. But the p.r. v.p. would be expected to work closely and regularly with the CEO—so closely and so regularly, writing speeches and preparing annual reports and so forth, that no one could be selected for the job without the CEO's review and approval. In this job my most important relationship, therefore, would be with my boss's boss's boss. To me it sounded like a recipe for getting shot to pieces if war broke out on executive row.

I had a number of interviews with Peter LiBasse. I found that he quickly and consistently slipped into an inquisitorial role, making it plain that he couldn't understand why I would consider leaving McDonnell Douglas for The Travelers. I stuck firmly to my script: I'd been with McDonnell Douglas for twelve years, I'd accomplished everything I was likely to accomplish there, and I'd decided that if I wasn't going to find myself stuck in the same rut for another fifteen or twenty years I'd better make a move soon. If I wanted something new, what could possibly make more sense than a switch from aerospace to one of the giants of the financial services industry? It would broaden my experience and give me new credentials. Et cetera et cetera, blah blah blah.

Wasn't I troubled by the thought of leaving the city where my family had lived for twenty years? Nah, not at all! My wife wasn't from St. Louis originally, both of us had lived happily in other places, we'd always found New England one of the most attractive places in the world, she felt as ready for new adventures as I did . . . blah blah blah.

Was I on the verge of a divorce? Was I in financial trouble? Did I have a police record of any kind? How about my kids—were my kids in trouble?

I just kept smiling and saying no no no, everything is fine. I have nothing to hide. If you need my permission to conduct a thorough investigation of my past or my finances or my family, just show me where to sign.

LiBasse was sufficiently satisfied to send me on to a breakfast meeting with the chairman of the board. It was, I know now, a typical CEO interview, which is to say that I can't remember a single interesting thing about it. Again my perceptions didn't mean anything, though: within twenty-four hours I got a call inviting me to return to Hartford for *dinner* with the chairman. I accepted, and after the two of us had spent a long evening trading clichés about the perfidy of the press and the power of the truth in winning the loyalty of employees I got still another call inviting me back one more time. It seemed virtually inevitable that on this trip they were going to make an offer. Victory was at hand.

How was I able to shuttle back and forth between St. Louis and Hartford this way? It was no problem, actually. Nobody in a position of authority at McDonnell Douglas cared what I did. The colonel, I'm sure, wished I were dead. To keep myself covered during my absences I kept in touch by phone with my old secretary, who would know if anybody was looking for me. Nobody ever was. So far as I know, nobody ever noticed that I was gone.

I was well into my long dance with The Travelers when a woman who was the J. I. Case Company's headhunter flew to St. Louis to look me over. She told me how the company had recently been in severe financial trouble—where had I heard *that* before?—but now had a dynamic new president and was in the early phases of what promised to be an astonishingly brilliant turnaround. Shortly after that, I was invited to fly to Chicago for an airport meeting with Case's top HR guy, who told me more about the turnaround and the things the new president was doing and the company's need for someone capable of building the kind of first-rate communications operation it was going to need on the way to becoming a first-rate corporation.

This led quickly to a second trip. In a suite of meeting rooms at O'Hare I was introduced to the new Case CEO, a trim, compact, dark-haired man of about fifty named Jim Ashford. He was interviewing a number of people that day—it was part of the process by which he was hurriedly rebuilding the company's entire management team, he told me—and so our talk was short and very much to the point. He told me that Case had lost a quarter of a billion dollars in 1987, and he explained why. He told me that within a few years the company was going to be turning a profit of at least half a billion dollars a year. Eventually, he said, it was going to be outperforming John Deere as a producer of farm equipment and Caterpillar as a producer of construction equipment. That was his mission. He asked short, specific, sensible questions about my experience and interests, and I gave him direct answers.

"Do you like international work?"

"I *love* it!"

Nothing that he asked required me—none of it even tempted me—to lie or exaggerate or conceal. Nothing made it necessary for me to pretend interest in things that didn't really interest me much at all. This was a surprise and a relief compared with the situations I'd encountered at Continental Bank and The Travelers.

After not much more than a half hour of talk Ashford, almost abruptly, excused himself. He was late for another interview, he said, and had another waiting after that. I wondered if he had lost interest in me that quickly. But then, almost immediately, his HR man came into the room smiling.

"Jim says you look like a good guy," he said. "He says we should get you if we can." After the endless flirtations at Continental Bank and The Travelers, I found such directness nearly unbelievable.

That November my cup ran over: The Travelers and J. I. Case both offered me jobs with salaries significantly higher than what

I'd been making at McDonnell Douglas. The two offers came within seventy-two hours of each other. After months of defeat and rejection and worry, suddenly I had the luxury of choosing, of being the one to say no—to somebody.

I looked at J. I. Case and saw an old, old company (founded as a producer of threshing machines in the early 1840s) that in recent years had been losing shocking amounts of money but was now owned by oil-and-gas-rich Tenneco Inc. of Houston, so that it had deep parental pockets from which to draw.

I saw a new president, Jim Ashford, who was said to be a star performer in tough situations, seemed to know exactly what he wanted, and clearly was going after it.

I saw a company that had major manufacturing facilities not just across the upper Midwest but in England, France, Germany, and Spain. If I signed on I could continue to travel the world and play at being an international wheeler-dealer.

When I looked at Case I also saw a small and amateurish communications department, one that Ashford said he wanted me to improve in a hurry. Thus I saw a chance to do something interesting, and in the process to contribute to the accomplishment of something worthwhile.

In looking at The Travelers, I saw the kind of old-line financial colossus that traditionally had offered total security but now was slipping deeper and deeper into the pit its own management had dug for it. I saw a top-heavy, involuted bureaucracy that didn't seem to have any goals and that had, for all I knew, chosen me for no better reason than the exhaustion resulting from a search that had gone on too long and the fact that I'd never been in trouble with MasterCard or the police.

When I looked at Case I saw the prospect of living in a drab rust-belt town—Racine, Wisconsin—that did, however, have certain attractions. It was on Lake Michigan, which is very nearly as good as being on the ocean. It was near Chicago and even nearer Milwaukee. It was just a six-hour drive from St. Louis and therefore from my son and parents and sister and friends.

When I looked at The Travelers I was faced with an almost

equally drab town a full thousand miles from the place Pam and I were likely to think of as home forever.

I sought out people whose judgment I respected. One was a Ph.D. economist and head of research at the Federal Reserve Bank of St. Louis. Another was an MBA/CPA with years of experience in manufacturing management. Mainly I asked them to help me with the question of whether J. I. Case was too big a risk—whether it was reasonable to expect that Ashford really could turn the operation around. What they told me was encouraging. Case's huge losses, they said, basically had two causes. One was the difficult, costly process of absorbing all the factories and distribution systems the company had bought from International Harvester when Harvester collapsed in the mid-eighties. The other was the deep depression into which American agriculture had fallen in the early eighties, with farmers going bankrupt by the hundreds of thousands and the survivors unable or unwilling to buy new machines. The absorption of International Harvester was a manageable problem, my friends told me; evidently the process of bringing it under control was already under way. The agricultural depression was over, the economist told me; from here on things were likely to get a lot better.

And so I called Peter LiBasse in Connecticut and told him that after a lot of thought, and without feeling certain that I was making the right choice, I had decided not to accept his offer. I found this hard; I've always found it excruciating to quit or to turn down jobs. LiBasse made it all the harder by being very gracious. He kept calling me "friend" and telling me how excited he'd been about the thought of my arrival.

And at sunset on December 4, 1988, I entered Wisconsin in a car crammed full of executive regalia and framed pictures for the walls of my new office. Off to my left an immense crimson wall was ablaze in the western sky. I drank it in and thought of the old seafaring prayer: Red sky at night, sailor's delight.

I hoped it was a harbinger of good things to come.

It wasn't.

PART VI

J. I. Case

Down and Out

54

From the beginning, in small ways at first and eventually in very big ways indeed, taking the job at J. I. Case turned out to be my ultimate mistake. At first it was merely a series of disappointments. Gradually the disappointments grew more serious. Finally they snowballed into an avalanche, a disaster. "Career-wise," as they say, I was buried.

The first, smallest, most trivial of the disappointments was the company's main office building. It was a ninety-year-old semi-wreck on a decrepit street in Racine, Wisconsin's semi-decrepit downtown. I was given an office next to the office of the president, Jim Ashford. Supposedly this was so that he and I could be in constant contact. Later I decided that it was because nobody else wanted to be so close. It was an office out of Dickens, small but with an immensely high ceiling and doors on three sides leading in equally useless directions. On its walls was a paneling that had been cheap when it was new and now was in various stages of coming down.

That was okay, really. That was acceptable. I'd been given a glimpse of the building before accepting the job. Though I hadn't seen enough to understand how bad it was, I recognized it as a fitting symbol of an exhausted organization urgently in need of rejuvenation. The building was the past; what mattered was what lay ahead. Jim Ashford had told me of his plans to erect a new headquarters complex. If working for a few years in an almost ludicrously dismal setting was part of the price of taking part in one of the most remarkable business stories of the 1990s, that was a price I was willing to pay. If we succeeded, I and all the other new people on Ashford's staff would have been part of something that really mattered. And we would be amply rewarded for doing so; the stock options in our compensation packages made that certain. A few years in an office slum wasn't too much to ask.

But nothing at Case turned out to be what I had expected. In the months before my arrival, Ashford had reorganized the company into five business units. Two of these, the agricultural equipment group and the construction equipment group, were the most important by far. Together they included more than twenty thousand employees, all of the company's manufacturing plants, and thousands of dealers on several continents. During my first few weeks in Racine I discovered that neither of these units had capable communications management, that both of them were using outside agencies to meet nearly all their communications needs, that the work of these agencies was virtually unsupervised, and that the company was, as a result, squandering astonishing sums of money.

Within a month of my arrival I outlined a plan for putting things right. We would get rid of the agencies and their astronomical bills, use some small part of the money saved to expand the staff, and let the bulk of the savings fall to the bottom line. I felt we could improve the quality of the work being done and in the process save at least half a million dollars a year. My own opinion was that we could probably save a million dollars a year, but I used the half-million figure to protect myself from promising too much. I told Ashford that I was prepared to take full responsibility for achieving both things: improved quality, lower costs. I expected an enthusiastic response; cost reduction and quality improvement were two of the things he always stressed when he talked about his goals for Case. And he always said emphatically that lower costs and higher quality weren't incompatible—that when you do things right you waste less time and money and get better results. I was, I thought, taking him at his word. I thought I was giving him exactly what he wanted.

I explained my plan to him face to face, in his office. He responded ambiguously, moving on to other subjects and leaving my idea hanging. Later I put it in writing and sent it to him as a memo. Weeks went by without any response. During those weeks I was learning that Ashford wasn't the sort of boss you could just drop in on for a talk. Just dropping in to see Jim Ashford, actually, was a lot like just dropping into a freezer. After about thirty seconds you were feeling the chill and looking for the door.

Because my office was next to Ashford's I was able to watch the comings and goings. I watched to see who *did* drop in on the boss and stay to shoot the bull. The answer soon became clear: nobody. Jim Ashford had no intimates, no pals, not even anybody he seemed comfortable with. Even his top lieutenants, the executive vice presidents, almost never set foot in his office. When they did they always left after a minute or two unless they were there to crunch numbers. And these, too, were men whom Ashford himself had recruited into the company.

It occurred to me that perhaps Ashford was worried about the political ramifications of what I was proposing—was afraid that the heads of his business units would resent or resist having their communications taken over by corporate staff. It was my memories of McDonnell Douglas that brought this to mind; turf wars had been a daily reality there, constantly draining energy out of the organization. And so, thinking that if there was a turf question the best thing was to confront it directly, I took my idea to the two people most likely to oppose it, the heads of the agricultural and construction equipment groups.

They responded eagerly, probably in part because they were under intense pressure to get their groups into the black. More for less was exactly what they needed, and it was exactly what I was offering. In short order we worked out an agreement under which I was to assume responsibility for the communications needs of their groups. They seemed even more delighted by the idea than I was.

Happily, eagerly, naively, I reported to Ashford on the deal I'd worked out. I did this by memo, having given up by this time on the possibility of sitting down and discussing anything with him. Again I described the benefits that I expected. While waiting for his reply I began to work out detailed plans for the rearrangement of staffs, assignments, budgets.

One evening about a week later Ashford came into my office with my memo in his hand. He waved it at me.

"I want you to forget this whole thing," he said.

Huh?

"I want you to stay away from the business units."

"But, Jim . . ."

"Do you hear what I'm saying?"

"Of course."

"Good." And he turned on his heel and was gone.

With that, all possibility of doing what I thought I'd been hired to do—putting the company's communications on a rational, professional, cost-effective footing—died an early death. I'd been in Wisconsin perhaps sixty days, and already my best reasons for coming were gone. I was left with a tiny staff of people who'd been demoralized by the company's problems and mismanagement long before my arrival, were freshly demoralized by my failure to win approval for even the simplest and most obviously necessary remedies, and were now barely capable of caring. I found myself in a job so small, handling assignments and responsibilities so trivial, that it shamed me to talk about them. Old friends in St. Louis would call and ask how things were going, and I'd tell them that everything was wonderful—great company, great boss, great job. This was easier than confessing that I'd torn my family's life up by its roots for a situation so confining, so heartbreaking, that if given a dose of truth serum I probably wouldn't have been able to find one good thing to say about it.

My only consolation was the knowledge that I wasn't alone in my disappointment: similar things were happening in every part of the company. Hopeless though he appeared to be in personal relationships, Ashford had an incongruous appetite for giving talks to assembled groups of workers. His talks were effective to an extent that amazed people who knew what he was like in the office. Whenever he found an audience, or whenever one was assembled for him, he would launch into passionate homilies about the company's urgent need for better quality, lower costs, more cooperation, people willing to take risks and accept responsibility—all the latest shibboleths of American management. But when the people who reported to him tried to put these buzz-words into practice, more often than not they found themselves ignored or overtly blocked. More than once, when I made furtive inquiries to find out why some senior executive no longer seemed to be around, I heard a story about how the missing man had been foiled by Ashford and had exploded in frustration and quit.

"To hell with you," one of them was supposed to have said. "This isn't what I signed up for." And he'd walked out on Ashford exactly the way Ashford had walked out on me.

I admired that kind of chutzpah. Part of me wished I had it. But I knew I didn't. With what in retrospect feels like astonishing foolishness, I already felt stuck in Racine. Pam and I, in exploring Racine when she was in town one weekend, had come upon a beautiful lakeside house for sale and had put money down on it. Pam had already given notice at her job, had helped her boss find a replacement, and was teaching the replacement to take over. If I quit now and went out looking for work yet again, how was I going to explain being unemployed in the aftermath of having been vice president of two different corporations in two different states in the space of the past ninety days?

Like a lot of the newcomers to Case, I hunkered down and hoped that things would improve—that Jim Ashford would commit suicide, maybe, or just go away.

It's a pathetic fact that by the time I'd been at Case six months all my aspirations were focused on a sheet of yellow graph paper that I kept in the top drawer of my desk. On this sheet I'd outlined sixty little squares, each square representing one month. Every time another month went by I'd take out the piece of graph paper and fill in one of the squares with black ink. In five years all the squares would be filled in. At that point I'd be vested: eligible to receive, someday, a little pension from Case to go with my little pension from McDonnell Douglas. I could see nothing more lofty to hope for. It was a good deal like being in prison, marking off the days. It was also a good deal like my early years at McDonnell Douglas, and like even earlier years at

Meredith Publishing Company. It was corporate life, in short. What was wrong with me, that I kept forgetting?

At the end of May Sarah graduated from high school, and early in June she and Pam arrived in Racine. Pam had landed a job as vice president of a small college ten miles from home. Characteristically, she had filled herself with enthusiasm for the new life that was starting. Other people were arriving in Racine, too—growing numbers of new Case vice presidents. The company gave every one of us a new Oldsmobile, a country club membership, a lavish relocation package, a salary big enough to lure good people away from bigger and healthier companies, and a bundle of stock options cashable upon completion of four years of service. There weren't enough houses in Racine for all these newcomers and their money. Real estate prices started to climb. Construction started to boom.

To me it seemed strange: such massive recruitment of scores of costly executive talent by a company that was supposedly hell-bent to cut costs, accompanied by a baffling refusal to let the new people do what they thought they'd been hired to do. But Jim Ashford had a history of successful turnarounds, albeit with smaller organizations. I had nothing of the kind. Jim Ashford had completed the Harvard Business School's Advanced Management Program, and I hadn't. It seemed reasonable that he knew what he was doing, that he was a better judge of these things than an old English major who'd never been president of anything.

Every Monday morning Ashford held a meeting of the eleven people who reported directly to him. Once a month all eleven of us would join him for an all-day operations review meeting. He'd sit at the head of the table in our shabby, windowless conference room, and one by one we'd report to him on what was happening in the parts of the company we were supposedly responsible for. The heads of the operating units would have to stand at the foot of the table, project their results and their forecasts on a screen, and explain. Ashford would observe silently. At the end of each presentation he would make his comments. Invariably he would complain that the numbers were unacceptable. Inventories were always higher than they'd been the month before, and he would repeat what he'd said the month before: that this absolutely had to stop. Head count, too, was always higher in all the units, and Ashford would complain about this as well. He would tell the unit heads that they had better come back with lower numbers next time. The unit heads would nod gravely and put their slides away. And a month later all the numbers would be higher again and we'd repeat the whole routine.

Oddly, the numbers questions seemed to come up only during these meetings. Between the meetings, as far as I could tell, Ashford never did anything to make sure that his instructions were being followed. Nor did the unit heads ever explain—I'm sure they'd say they never had a real chance to explain—why the numbers weren't improving. I clung to the belief that surely Ashford had to know what he was doing. I assumed that I just didn't understand—that the whole thing couldn't possibly be half as bad as it looked.

I spoke as little as possible at these meetings. I had nothing to speak *about*. The business units were spending millions on advertising and marketing communications, and though I was the only one in the room who knew much about such things, I'd been forbidden to get involved in the situation. I had a monthly employee newspaper to run and an annual report to produce and some generally trivial media relations and community relations projects to worry about and not much else. At meetings dealing with millions and hundreds of millions and sometimes billions of dollars, what I was doing in my job looked so petty, so childish almost, that I cringed at the thought of describing it. What Ashford had in mind when he'd hired me, what he thought justified my salary now that I was here—these things were beyond imagining.

Life at Case was punctuated with disappearances. Some of the most important people in the company hierarchy would be with us on Thursday, gone forever on Friday. And none of it was ever explained. One of the two executive vice presidents who had agreed to my reorganization plan was fired immediately after playing a lead role in one of our monthly operating reviews; I learned about it when he called from home that evening to say good-bye. "This just isn't working out," he said, was the only explanation Ashford had offered. The other executive vice president had been fired in a similar way even earlier. For a while two senior vice presidents, also newcomers to Case, were elevated into the vacant spots. Eventually they too were fired. This sort of thing was happening almost constantly, in every part of the company and at every level. And all the while more and more new recruits were being brought in to fill the pipeline, and none of what was happening was ever explained. Even the grapevine never seemed to know. In the midst of all the carnage, I, with little to do, was left unmolested. At the end of every month I would fill in another square and hope for the best.

I couldn't go job hunting: I'd only recently scoured the country looking for a job. I'd been at Case only months. Once or twice I got calls from headhunters, but though I always responded eagerly nothing ever came of them.

People at Case became desperate to prove their value. Despite a total lack of evidence that doing so would make any difference, they began to compete to see who could arrive for work first and stay longest. Twelve-hour days became commonplace, Saturdays at the office the norm. I began to hear about meetings scheduled for seven o'clock on Sunday mornings. I knew of one vice president who sat at his desk all day every Saturday with a novel in his lap, pretending to work but catching up on Ken Follett.

I contented myself with arriving before Ashford every morning and staying at my desk until he was gone every night. That wasn't hard at all. Jim Ashford's workdays tended to be as short as they were unsweet.

In the one area I felt capable of judging, communications, most of the things the company was doing continued to be done badly and at three, four, even five times what they should have cost. Occasionally the waste became astronomical. An all too typical example was the fancy multicolor slides that Ashford liked to use when he had to give a presentation. A graphic designer who reported to me was responsible for the production of these slides, and because he didn't have the equipment needed to make them in his office, the work had to be farmed out. That wouldn't have been a big problem except for the fact that Ashford and the people who helped him prepare his presentations invariably kept changing and rechanging things until literally the last minute. When you do that with multicolor slides, you reach a point at which the job can't be done in time for the presentation unless your outside contractors work all night to get it done. And when you're at that point, the contractors have you at their mercy. Their charges go into the stratosphere. During my first year with Case we spent unthinkable sums—hundreds of thousands of dollars—on the production of quite ordinary slides. The slides for a single presentation to a group of security analysts, redone for the last time on an emergency overnight basis, ended up costing sixty thousand dollars—the price of a Mercedes—for one tray of slides that were used only once. But when I requested permission to buy a sixteen-hundred-dollar piece of equipment that would have made it possible for us to produce our own slides—overnight, if necessary—at a cost of six cents each, I was told that there was no money for such foolishness. This in a company where employees were constantly being warned that our survival was dependent on our ability to cut costs and "work smarter."

Nobody talked about these things around the office. Everybody was afraid of Ashford. Away from the premises, people who trusted one another talked plenty. An executive vice president told me that Jim Ashford made him think of Saddam Hussein.

Frequently in the early months, far less frequently as the months went by, I would send written suggestions and requests and recommendations into Ashford's office. Perhaps a third of the time at first, less often later, he would approve or agree or give his consent—almost always in connection with something that didn't matter much. A third of the time he would say no, always without explanation. The rest of the time he wouldn't answer at all. Somewhere between a third and half of all the suggestions I sent him might just as well have been torn into tiny pieces and thrown out the window. It's possible, of course, that the fault was all mine, that there was something intolerably wrong with my memos or my ideas. He never said so, though. He never said anything about them.

One of the things I inherited upon arriving at Case was a wretched employee newspaper that never came out on time and rarely contained any news that mattered. This was one of the few things I found it possible to control, and so I replaced the editor, introduced a new design, and began to upgrade the content. I cared enough about this (it was very nearly my only opportunity to accomplish anything) to corner Ashford in his office one day and more or less force him to discuss it with me.

We need to tell employees something about what's going on in this company, I said. We need to tell them what you want and what you think. We need a message from the president. If you'll agree, I'll write the message for you. You just give me one topic a month—whatever you think is important that month—and I'll take care of the rest.

He consented. Consenting got me out of his office.

But when I would ask him for subjects, for things he wanted employees to know or believe or do, he almost never had any to offer. And so I stole ideas from his occasional lectures to employees, from business magazines, from wherever I could find them. I'd write a president's message and give it to his secretary with the request that she try to get his approval. Usually what I'd written came back with a tiny "OK" penciled at the top in his hand. Two of them, though, came back with this message: "I think you had better find a different topic." He offered no suggestions. Finding a different topic was no concern of his, obviously.

Things were darkening for Pam, too. Her new boss, the president of the college where she was working, was in his own way even more difficult than Ashford. He communicated, but when he did so it was to express demands, expectations that she could see no way of satisfying. Work was becoming hellish for both of us at the same time. Evenings at home became a time for nursing ourselves back to a point where we had enough strength to go back the next morning for one more try.

Ashford liked to visit the factories and give his pep talks, and so a couple of times each month he'd climb aboard one of the company's executive jets and fly off to Burlington, Iowa, or Fargo, North Dakota, or East Moline, Illinois, or whatever spot he'd chosen. With him he'd take whoever at headquarters was responsible for the factory he'd decided to favor. During these visits he was bonhomie personified, walking up and down assembly lines shaking hands, giving lunchtime talks to gatherings of junior managers, visiting the offices to flirt with the secretaries. Then at the end of the day, trailing his traveling companion behind him, he'd return to the airport for the flight back to Racine. And as soon as they were on board Ashford would pull an invisible wall around himself. For the length of the flight he'd have nothing to say—nothing. His lieutenants, needless to say, were unnerved by this the first time they experienced it. Then they would learn that everybody got the same treatment, and they'd make their adjustments. Like a good many other strange things, it became part of the routine at J. I. Case.

One of the executive vice presidents, the one who ran the agricultural equipment group and therefore was the second most important executive in the company, looked back through his calendar after being fired and added up all the time he'd spent with Ashford in direct one-on-one discussion of business issues during his last ten months with the company. The cumulative total for those ten months, January through October 1990, turned out to be fifty minutes. Five minutes per month, on average, during a crucial year. Case was a weak and troubled company faced with almost overwhelming competition and presumably in the midst of a massive overhaul, and for all practical purposes its top people never talked with one another.

Somehow, somewhat strangely in retrospect, Case really did seem to be pulling off a turnaround of historic dimensions during my first two years there. In 1987—a year that ended with one president being fired and Ashford being sent in as his replacement—the company lost two hundred and fifty million dollars. In 1988, the year when I and a flood of other recruits reported for duty, the loss was ninety million dollars—still a calamity, but a big improvement all the same. In 1989 the company didn't merely turn profitable but earned two hundred and thirty million dollars. Thus it had achieved an improvement of nearly half a billion dollars in just two years. When this became known it was rumored inside the company and reported in the business press that Jim Ashford would soon be going to Houston to become the head of Tenneco, Case's mighty parent. This, I think, is why some very talented senior executives stayed at Case despite its bizarre president. They reasoned that Ashford would soon be gone, I suspect, and reasoned further that if he didn't fire them before departing they might have a shot at succeeding him.

How could such a troubled company make such rapid progress under a man like Jim Ashford? No doubt the reasons are many and complex. I can offer a few. One is the fact that many of the people brought into the company were quite able and worked very hard; in some areas they brought about impressive improvements with surprising speed. Another reason is that in 1989 and through most of 1990 the company had a strong wind at its back. Construction activity was still at the high levels of the eighties in North America and Europe and other parts of the world, and so construction equipment was selling briskly. And agriculture came back, just as my economist friend had said it would. Farmers started buying tractors and combines and other machines at the fastest rate in years. Ashford increased the production rate at most of the company's factories, per-unit costs fell as a result, and the profit on every unit sold jumped upward. The money rolled in, and everybody was in a hurry to celebrate. Tenneco, our mother corporation, sent its shareholders a financial report featuring the improvement at Case. "Here comes the harvest!" said its cover.

With things seeming to go so well—and who was I to argue, with professional financial analysts encouraging investors to buy our stock?—we decided that Pam, at least, could afford to get out. She quit her job, turned down an offer of a new one, and started down her father's old road: selling insurance. For the first time in a long time we were dependent almost entirely on my salary.

To some extent—the available evidence indicates that it was a great extent—the improvement in Case's performance was a fiction, something that existed only on paper. The rules that govern accountancy in the U.S. allow manufacturing companies to calculate their sales and profits in ways that are sometimes strange to the lay observer. When a company such as Case builds a tractor or a bulldozer or some other piece of machinery, that piece of machinery can be recorded as sold—and a profit from the sale can be entered in the books—as soon as it has been delivered to a dealer. This is called a wholesale sale, and it's perfectly legal if also somewhat peculiar by the standards of everyday common sense. Some part of the handsome profits that Case was reporting in the late 1980s and the beginning of the 1990s reflected nothing more substantial than the speed with which the company was building products and shipping them off to dealers around the world. Those products were piling up unsold on dealer lots in dangerous numbers. As the markets weakened in early 1991—the first sign of the coming big recession—the number of unsold machines mounted. So did the paper profits.

If sales had continued to expand Case might have eventually worked down its inventory of finished products and brought its predicament under control. That, presumably, was what the people making the decisions—Ashford and the Tenneco CEO he was expected to succeed—gambled on. Ashford, I know from personal experience, was by the end of 1991 lashing out angrily at subordinates who reported that it simply was not possible to sell all the machinery the company was producing.

"That's what you're being paid to do," he would say in a low and angry voice after listening to the laments of his minions. "You and your people are being paid to *sell*. And you can tell your people for me that if they can't do it, we'll find somebody who can."

His lectures didn't help. The economy was slipping, and sales continued to fall.

And Tenneco, all this time, was continuing to tell investors that everything was fine. Better than fine. "Here comes the harvest."

Agricultural and construction equipment markets continued to deteriorate at an alarming rate, not just in the U.S. but around the world, not just for Case but for every producer. When equipment did sell it was at a discount, so that the wholesale profits previously booked weren't covered by the cash actually received. The senior manufacturing and sales and financial people at Case were telling Ashford that production had to be cut. Ashford was refusing. He was making what now appears to have been a desperate dash for the finish line. In January he was named executive vice president of Tenneco and a member of its board of directors. Tenneco people in Houston told me that he and his wife had been seen shopping for a house there. People said it was only a matter of months—of weeks, possibly—until his elevation. Then, safely entrenched as a grand potentate at the top of the parent company, he would be free to blame his successor at Case when the avalanche came down.

In March the head of Human Resources of Case told me that an announcement about Ashford was imminent, that I would be given twenty-four hours to prepare a press release, and that I was to say nothing to anyone. I didn't even tell Pam. I assumed that the announcement would involve new glories for Ashford.

The secret, when it was revealed to me, was unexpected. My instructions were to prepare an announcement of Ashford's departure from Case, from Tenneco, from the whole mess. Again there were no explanations, not in the beginning and not later.

When Ashford was gone I was left with no boss, no message, no one to invent messages for. I hung on, hoping for the appointment of a new president, hoping that the new president when he arrived would care about communications. With the right new president, one with a real rescue plan and a desire to communicate that plan to employees and the outside world, my job could conceivably be worth doing for the first time since my arrival.

One of the Tenneco big shots flew in from Houston one day and gathered the Ashford staff in the conference room. He told us not to worry. "We're very aware that with the company's present problems we could never attract a management team the equal of this one," he said. "We need you. We want to keep you. You have nothing to worry about."

Liar liar pants on fire. From that day the disappearance of the members of Ashford's former staff members proceeded more rapidly than ever.

A month went by with no announcement of a new president. Word started to leak through the company about how much trouble we actually were in. People were talking about losses in the hundreds of millions of dollars. You could feel the panic, and nobody was in charge. I'd never seen a situation in which communication was needed so badly, or in which less effort was being made to communicate anything.

Another month went by, and still we had no president. The talk now was about a loss of hundreds of millions of dollars, not for the year but in a single *quarter*. People by the thousands were wondering what was going to happen, where the company was going, whether their jobs were going to last another year or another month. And still nobody was telling them anything. If we get a president who knows what he's doing, I kept telling myself, there's going to be a world of work for me.

Layoffs were accelerating at all levels, by the hundreds and then thousands of people. And then one June morning I got a call telling me that the top guy in Human Resources needed to see me. As soon as I'd sat down in his office he started talking fast about how sorry he was but the company was hemorrhaging from every orifice and they just had to cut way back and my whole department was being wiped out and there was nothing he could do about it there just wasn't a job for me anymore sorry sorry sorry.

And that was that. My second firing in thirty-six months. The start of another job search. This time, though, I was being sent out into the market a badly damaged piece of merchandise.

After I was gone a group of shareholders filed suit. They claimed that Ashford, the chairman of Tenneco, and Tenneco itself had cheated them by concealing Case's problems. They collected fifty million dollars in an out-of-court settlement.

And the recession went on and on and on, looking more and more like something too big to be called a mere recession, and the layoffs everywhere went on and on too.

And the forests of America were carted off to make paper for our résumés.

PART VII

1995
Consolation

55

THE TEN J. I. Case Company vice presidents who were called together and assured that they need not worry about their jobs?

Within a year they were gone to the last man. And not voluntarily.

The colonel who replaced me at McDonnell Douglas? Himself replaced before very long.

The man who took the job I declined at Travelers Insurance—gone within a few years.

Even Dr. M. Blakeman Ingle, the president of Imcera Group. Gone. Removed by the chairman he'd been chosen to succeed.

Bob retired to the Carolinas. D moved away and left no address. M ended up with a small company way up on the eastern shore of Lake Michigan. R never found a job anywhere. S bought a Mail Boxes franchise. Jim Ashford became the head of an auto parts company an hour south of Detroit.

And in the months that followed I saw more and more people like these lose their places in the corporate world and fail completely to find new ones.

Continental Bank was taken over by another company. Gerber Products was taken over by another company. Even The Travelers, with all its vast size, was taken over by another company. And with every such takeover, more and more people were scattered, were downsized, to the four points of the compass.

This too has gone on month after month after month. Downsizing has taken on a logic of its own—has lost its connection to takeovers or to financial problems or even to genuine business need. Sara Lee: nearly ten thousand jobs gone at the stroke of a pen. American Express: six thousand jobs will be gone by 1996.

Just months ago Mattel Inc., the toymaker, made what has become an unsurprising kind of announcement. It said it had record sales and record profits in 1994. That it was increasing its dividend and splitting its stock. And that in the midst of this bounty it was eliminating one thousand jobs.

Life is hard. Life has turned out to be vastly harder than I was taught to expect at St. Mark's School or McBride High. I did my best to make a career for myself, Pam and I did our best to build a family and center it upon a permanent home, and in the end it came down to all of us putting our things into cardboard boxes and going our separate ways.

Sometimes life seems to be exactly what the most terrible words in Shakespeare say it is. A tale told by an idiot. Full of sound and fury. Signifying nothing. I turn these words over in my mouth and imagine a madman with disheveled hair and a crushed spirit yelling them into the void.

I believe them, though.

Life is beautiful and good. At times life seems so rich I think my heart is going to burst open like some great ripe tropical fruit. The littlest things in the world, the things we see and hear and feel and smell almost without noticing, even they are almost enough to justify everything. The big things, the things so big we can't get to the bottom of them no matter how we try, make the simple act of being alive an infinitely valuable gift.

I believe that, too.

I don't see how it's possible to be satisfied with any explanation of life that doesn't embrace both perspectives, the dark one and the bright. This has to be what Chesterton meant when he said we have to love the world without trusting it. Trying to deny either half, the dark or the bright, does not work. Settling for half—for either half—is for children.

When I began this chronicle I thought I was recording the misadventures of a middle-aged white male out of work in a bad recession. Now I realize I was dealing with something very different from a recession, something that hasn't gone away even now that interest rates are climbing crazily instead of falling crazily and the economic indicators have all turned up. The recession is history. Downsizing goes on and on. The smashing of the certainties on which we used to build our lives goes on and on and on.

When I began this chronicle I wondered how it would end. Triumphantly, with me in some wonder job? Horribly, with my life and family in a terminal shambles? In some way none of us could possibly have foreseen—some ironic or hilarious or profoundly meaningful way?

Now at last I understand something we've all been hearing since childhood: that the true stories of real human beings don't have an end this side of the grave. Pam heard somebody say it this way: "Closure is the fantasy of a passive life." It's now more than six years since I fled McDonnell Douglas, more than three years since I was thrown out of J. I. Case, and I still wonder how it's going to end.

Predictably, my work with the Cushman agency in Chicago came to a bad end quite quickly. Century 21 first shrugged me off, later changed agencies altogether. We tried to get new clients but didn't have the credentials needed to impress the kinds of big ones we needed; pitches to possible clients became a nerve-wracking and doomed process of pretending to be what we weren't. Besides Aaron Cushman himself and president Tom Amberg, I was the highest-paid member of the staff. Predictably, properly, inevitably, I was let go.

But at exactly that point, as the result of an ad I'd answered almost without thought or hope, I was hired as director of communications by Marquette University in Milwaukee, a tolerable commute from Racine. In pay and prestige the job was a big step down, but I was grateful for it. I enjoyed being at a university. I found things to do that seemed worth doing, and I worked hard. And after sixteen months I was let go. The two Jesuit priests who ran the place offered no explanation. They'd been firing people regularly—nearly all the deans, and administrators by the platoon—all the time I was there. Always without explanation. When my turn came they said only that they "felt it was time for a change." My own opinion, which they are free to contradict if they wish, is that they hired me in the fatuous belief that my background in big business had endowed me with magical powers. I think they expected me to use dark secrets from the corporate sanctum sanctorum to make Marquette, despite its total lack of distinction, as famous as Harvard—as famous as Notre Dame at a minimum. They were worshipers of big business, the Jesuits who ran Marquette; the president had an MBA from Stanford, said his fantasy was to own a creme-colored Rolls-Royce, and was the only priest I'd ever known to wear pin-striped suits. That, I think, is why they fired so many people—because that was what they saw big business doing. They wanted to be just like the big boys. I got them into a trio of *New York Times* stories and thought that was pretty good. I got them on the front page of *The Wall Street Journal*—even got the president's picture there—and thought it was almost a miracle. But then I was out of tricks. When it became clear that I possessed only tricks and no true magic, hard work was not enough to save me.

That seemed the end of the road, and it almost broke me. Mass mailing to headhunters, days spent calling to build a network—all of it seemed futile in the case of someone with a record as ruined as mine now was. And even *The Wall Street Journal* was reporting, by then, that networking was an idea whose time had gone—that the people who still had jobs were by now so sick of getting calls from the out-of-work that it wasn't worth the trouble. And so I didn't even try. Instead I got serious about buying a franchise. I embarked upon a study of the duct-cleaning business, and of Subway sandwich shops.

But just at that point, almost unbelievably, I was called by an Ohio headhunter named Mark Elliott, who had been given my name by a colleague who for some reason had it on file in Texas. Over the phone, sick of pretending and sick of hoping, I laid out for Elliott the whole humiliating tale of the past several years. I was surprised, after this, when he said he was flying out to meet me. Face to face I went through the whole story again, this time in greater detail. I was again surprised when he said he wanted me to meet his client.

As a result, for more than a year now I have been in a job I like very much with a company I like very much on the outskirts of Cleveland. The pay is less than at J. I. Case, a good deal more than at Marquette. There's a vast amount of work to be done, and decent, capable people to do it with. I have a larger staff than I had even at McDonnell Douglas, and my days are genuinely interesting.

Pam too has found a demanding job that she finds worth doing, and she too likes this place. The kids are in three different states, but are doing well and are, I think, happy.

Is this deliverance? I no longer believe in deliverance. The industry I'm working in has long been among the most regulated in the country. Now it's in the early stages of what is expected to be rapid and radical deregulation. My company and its competitors are downsizing, restructuring, preparing for hard times. No one knows for sure what is going to happen, or when. I hope I will be here a long time. I expect nothing.

For the time being it is enough to have been given this unexpected chance—this last chance, surely—to do my best with work that matters. That's exactly what I am trying hard to do: my best. I spend eleven hours a day at the office and take a full briefcase with me when I go home. It doesn't seem pointless. If my company succeeds we will save jobs. Families, possibly.

When I think back on everything that has happened, this is my main consolation.

That I have always tried to do my best.

There is comfort of a sort in the thought that I don't know what more I possibly could have done.